Hand Me
My Pink Furry Slipper—

I'm Going To Heaven!

Joyfully,
Dear Nancy
Laurette Connelly
♡

by Laurette M. Connelly

Hand Me My Pink Furry Slipper— I'm Going To Heaven!

Copyright © 1998
by
Laurette M. Connelly

Library of Congress Number: 98-65821

International Standard Book Number: 1-883294-70-3

Masthof Press
R.R. 1, Box 20, Mill Road
Morgantown, PA 19543-9701

Dedication

THIS BOOK IS LOVINGLY DEDICATED TO
ALL MY GRANDCHILDREN,
WHO ARE THE JOY OF MY LIFE.

SPECIAL THANKS TO
PEG, SCOTT, EDITH, DIAN, JOYCE,
MARY ANN, BRUCE, AND ALL THE FRIENDS
WHO ENCOURAGED ME TO PERSEVERE.

Table of Contents

Foreword

A question.
    A struggle.
        More questions.
            More struggles.
                Help from true believers.
            The Bible.
        An answer.
    Many answers.
PEACE.

Looking back, most of us Christians would probably admit we traveled this route. Oh, the vehicles in which we rode were different, but our internal experiences were similar. The good news, however, is that we all ended up at the same place: the foot of the cross. There we put our faith in the Lord Jesus Christ, who loved us enough to die in our stead that we might enjoy a relationship with Him forever.

In addition to our road of faith, we travelers have something else in common. We love to tell our horror stories, the "with-all-the-detours-and-roadblocks-I-don't-know-how-I-ever-got-here" stories. In this book Laurette Connelly tells hers quite humorously. In the following pages you will meet a warm, bubbly woman who has a heart for God. Not only that, she has a passion to introduce others to the Savior she now knows personally. Her zeal is so effusive it's contagious!

Although I (thankfully) am not one of the "characters" in her book, especially the one whose false eyelashes run the risk of getting caught on the tiny screws on her eyeglasses, I was in every scene as I read. In fact, once I opened the book, I couldn't put it down. What ridiculous situation would the author find herself in this time, and how would she get out of it? What question would she struggle with next, and how would it be resolved? Would I laugh or cry as I turned the page? I was prepared to do either—or both. I was never disappointed.

As this gifted author lets you into her world, savor every minute. Giggle with her as she giggles at herself. Then get serious as she fights her spiritual battles. Don't start reading just yet though. You will need a cup of coffee, a snuggle robe, and oh, yes—slippers. Once prepared, you'll be in for a treat. And you'll get it—Connelly style.

> - Peg Rankin, author of *Yet Will I Trust Him* and *How to Care for the Whole World and Still Take Care of Yourself*

Introduction

This book is not intended to be a historical narrative. It is a fictional account of factual events in my life. Most of the names have been changed to protect the innocent, of course.

My purpose for writing this book is to present simple answers to basic questions that someone may have in their search for Biblical truth. Having myself gone through a process of seeking, I have felt the pain and insecurity of confusion. I do not pretend to have all the answers, but my source is always and only the Bible. It is my hope that the reader will not see me pointing an accusing finger at any particular denomination, since I know that Christians may be found in a wide variety of churches. Rather, I hope that I have been successful in answering questions where I am certain they exist.

Scripture references are taken from the New International Version published by Zondervan, Inc.

CHAPTER ONE

Am I having fun yet?

"Me?—A sinner?—Do you really believe that?" I could feel the fury rising up within me as I stood face to face with my fifteen-year-old freckle-faced son, David. All of a sudden, he had religion and I was a sinner! Fifteen years I'd been teaching him and now he was going to be the teacher? Over my dead soul!!!

David had brought a Bible into the house. Like Mary's little lamb, everywhere that David went the Bible was sure to go. He was beginning to get on my nerves. When he started to use that Bible to accuse me of being a sinner, the mother-son relationship began to totter on the edge of disaster.

"Where do you get off calling me a sinner? Did someone die and make you pope?" I was stirring devil's food cake with a vengeance, shaking the wooden spoon at him and splattering him with chocolate. "Listen, honey, maybe you're a sinner, but I have seven children; I don't have time to sin!"

"But Mom, the Bible says . . . "

"Look, I don't want to hear what the Bible says!—Who do you think you are that you can interpret the Bible?" I was two paces behind him, my pink furry slippers flopping up and down on my feet. My adolescent-looking pony tail was bouncing menacingly from side to side with each step. I wanted to frost his head with chocolate batter. How could he make me this angry? This new found faith of his was doing nothing but causing anxieties and division in the family.

"A few months of Bible study and you're an authority on Scripture. Give me a break!" But David was undaunted. He just quietly shook his head and shuffled away, stripping off his sweaty track uniform as he headed for his room. "All right, Mom, if that's the way you feel, I guess I can't talk to you about this. But you can't stop me from praying for you."

Praying for me . . . Praying for me?—Now he'd done it! . . . I slammed the bowl down on the countertop, sending batter flying in every direction. I went barreling toward his room, swung the door open, and stood there momentarily speechless, as I found him on his knees.

I could feel my blood pressure rising. "I don't need your holier-than-thou prayers," I shouted venomously. My voice was beginning to tremble. I knew I was losing control. "I don't want to change. You may look at me and see a sinner. That's your problem! I like the way I am and so does your father and my friends as well. Don't waste your time praying for me to turn from what I believe. If you're on a mission to make a convert, why don't you find yourself a real sinner like Mrs. Blumm down the street who's always having an affair with someone's husband. Now there's a blatant sinner for you. That woman needs prayer. Do me a favor . . . make her your project and get off my case."

Tears began welling up in David's eyes. He'd always been gentle and tenderhearted. How could this sweet child suddenly have the power to elicit such a response from me? I was angry with him and with myself for allowing myself to be drawn into this kind of confrontation. Most of all, I was angry with people who were teaching him doctrines that were obviously contrary to what I had taught him, contrary to what I myself had been taught.

David had become involved in a "Young Life" group in school. It seemed harmless at the time, maybe even a positive influence in his life. But now I was having second thoughts. What were they filling his head with? I put my cake in the oven and sat down with a cigarette and a cup of coffee to try to compose myself.

2

The vision of seeing David on his knees made my thoughts flash back twelve years earlier to when he was a very shy three-year-old. I was sitting in Sister Superior's somber office interviewing for an assignment as a CCD (Confraternity of Christian Doctrine) teacher. As I sat across the desk from Sister Saint Agnes, little David just stood meekly beside me clinging to my skirt. Sister's long black habit and head covering were a little frightening to me. He refused to look at her. Suddenly, he spotted the large cross with a life-sized body of Christ hanging on the wall across the room. Without a word, he courageously let go of my skirt, walked over and knelt sweetly before the cross. He blessed himself, whispered a silent prayer, blessed himself again and resumed his position beside me. He hung on tightly to my skirt, maybe a little afraid I might be considering leaving him here with this mysterious stranger who was only partially visible in her long black robe and stiff starched headdress.

Sister had given me "carte blanche" to teach whatever I wanted. We'd been discussing all the possibilities. Since it was the month of May, I might consider teaching devotions to Mary our Blessed Mother as Queen of Heaven, devotions to the immaculate heart of Mary. Or since this class would be next year's confirmation class when these children would become soldiers in Christ's army, perhaps it might be best to begin reviewing confirmation questions. Another possibility was to go back to teaching basic catechism and Catholic doctrine.

All of it seemed rather unimportant as we gazed in awe at this little child innocently kneeling at the foot of the cross. Sister watched in startled disbelief. She was obviously impressed. She was convinced that if I had trained my children so well, I was without doubt a qualified teacher. By the end of the semester, I would surely have the entire class kneeling reverently in prayer. But I was puzzled. We, as a family, had never been in the habit of praying in front of a crucifix, yet something had inexplicably drawn this child to his knees. What could it be?

I was still pondering on the past when I heard music on David's tape player, "'Tis so sweet to walk with Jesus, step by step and day by day." This tune was catchy and I had no argument with the words, but something inside me was churning.

I walked back to my messy kitchen, tears streaming down my face, feeling ashamed, angry, confused. Whatever happened to my sense of wonder at this child who had never given me an ounce of trouble? What had happened to my sense of humor? Why was this so upsetting to me? I couldn't explain it, but I knew that dwelling on it for too long could be dangerous.

David's motivation was admirable. He'd found something he felt was worth sharing. There was no question that he loved me and I loved him. Hopefully, we'd make our peace before the day was over.

When my very tired redheaded husband arrived home from work to a clean kitchen and the smell of freshly baked chocolate cake, everything appeared rather normal and tranquil, at least on the surface. John gave me the usual bear hug while our frantically excited Irish setter, Manfred, tried to nuzzle his way between us. John set down his overflowing briefcase (he probably planned to spend the evening working again), loosened his tie, and plopped into his favorite lazy boy chair with a weary sigh. "Let me hear the sound of those ice cubes clinking in the glass. Whew, what a day!" Cocktail hour was indisputably the most relaxing part of our day. Usually we did most of our talking between sips of vodka and tonic. After dinner it was fairly predictable that he would either fall asleep watching sports on TV or he would be totally immersed in homework.

Sometimes it seemed to me that I was raising our seven children by myself. John's business had always required extensive traveling when the family was young, but it was easier then. Now that they were all between the ages of fifteen and twenty-five, the problems and demands on my time were magnified. Much of my day seemed to be spent in our red VW van.

"Why don't I need a license to do all the things I do?" I complained. "I'm a chauffeur, nurse, barber, hairdresser, coach, butler, cook, vet, seamstress, maid, teacher, counselor, butcher, baker, and candlestick maker. This family doesn't need me, they need a staff!"

Tonight, I needed to vent and I expected John's support. "Your youngest son and I had *some* kind of run-in today," I said, as I lit another cigarette to enjoy with my cocktail. "You know this religion thing is getting a little out of hand. He makes statements that are downright hurtful."

"I wouldn't make too much of it. Some of the other kids have gone through different phases, but they got over them. He will too. He'll outgrow it. Have you forgotten that you once planned to become a nun?" John laughed, reminding me that being Sister Saint Laurette had once been a very real goal of mine. I'd gone as far as going for interviews in different religious orders.

However, by the time I was seventeen, I had shelved the whole idea. I had worn long cotton stockings, orthopedic shoes, and a long-sleeved black habit with an itchy white collar all through my school years. I couldn't handle the same for the rest of my life. So much for my dedication. When they changed the rules and allowed nuns to wear fashionable clothing, maybe I'd reconsider. By the time the fashion industry reached the convent doors and you couldn't tell the nuns from the moms, I had seven children and they would never have accepted me. Though at times I was tempted to try.

"Get me to a nunnery!!!!" I would shout in exasperation. "I was born to be a Mother Superior . . . not a real mother!"

"Becoming a nun is one thing," I answered flippantly, annoyed at the comparison, "but nuns are not always pushing their beliefs on other people and they're not always preaching. They know how to have fun. Nobody knows how to party better than your cousin Lucy, and she's been a nun for thirty years. Do you know that David thinks I'm a sinner and so are you? Why, I wouldn't be surprised if he even thought cousin Lucy was a sinner."

John's hysterical laughter sent vodka and tonic spurting all over his paisley tie and dark gray pin-striped suit. "I always thought sinning would be more fun than this . . . Hey, if we've got the name, let's play the game. What do you say, let's go break into someone's house tonight," he howled.

"I think the McKenzies next door are away, and I have the key; we could start there. Betty has a few pieces of jewelry and a fur or two I wouldn't mind having," I added mockingly. "Then we could go see a dirty movie, and come home and beat the kids. Sounds like a perfect evening, doesn't it?"

By now we were both feeling a bit giggly and the whole situation didn't seem quite so intimidating. Maybe John was right, David would get through his pious phase just as I had. Then he'd be like any other kid, *normal.*

Of course, I had always wanted religion to have a place in my children's lives. But unless he wore a Roman collar, we could do without the sermonizing. However, if David was planning on going into the priesthood, that would be a different story. I could relate to that. I would someday be the proud mother of *Father David Connelly.* After all, wasn't that every Catholic mother's dream?

I could still see Father Morin climbing slowly up the dozen steps into the high pulpit covered with something that looked like a giant clam shell. He was so high above the congregation that anyone sitting in the first ten rows would end up with muscle spasms in the neck after the first five minutes. The vision of Father looking down ominously on his attentive subjects made his booming voice seem overwhelmingly authoritative. "God would never let the mother of a priest suffer the pains of hell. No, not after she's raised a son for him. Without a doubt, the mother of a priest is heaven bound!"

Wow! I'd have it made. I could ride on David's coattails. "I'm Father Connelly's mother, " I would announce proudly when I got to heaven's gate. "I believe my son has made a reservation for me. It's probably under his name. That would be Connelly with two n's and two l's."

By the time David was a senior in high school, his commitment to walking with the Lord was still growing in intensity. He was taking longer shaking his Bible-reading habit than I had in shaking the nun's habit. His shabby-looking Bible still followed him everywhere he went. For the last two summers he'd attended "Young Life Camp" and now he'd become a counselor. He was attending Bible study at least once a week. He listened mostly to Christian music and dated only Christian girls. What next? What had they done to my David?

Amazingly, he still managed to be fairly popular with his peers. The kids liked him. What's more, he was having fun. I guess I really had nothing to complain about. Some parents were up in arms because their kids were involved in wild drinking or pot parties week after week. But David and his friends would gather twenty and thirty strong to play silly games like indoor hide 'n' go seek. They laughed till they rolled on the floor in tears. They ordered pizza and cokes and asked the Lord's blessing before devouring them like the hungry teenagers they were.

To watch their behavior, you'd almost believe you'd been zapped back in time to the late forties when the living was easy and the pressures were simple and few. I had to admit, these were special kids. But I didn't understand the things they talked about. "All have sinned and fall short of the glory of God," they said.

"Honestly, lighten up," I thought.

One evening after a particularly large group had come to visit, I was helping David straighten up. There were napkins, cups, papers, and books from one end of the den to the other. "Where do you get that stuff about everyone being a sinner?" I asked gingerly, almost afraid to ignite a spark of agitation. I had so often cut him short that I wasn't sure he was willing to answer me anymore.

"That's what the Bible says, Mom. We're not making this stuff up."

"But David, the Bible wasn't meant to be taken literally. Of course, we all commit sins now and then. We're human, but that doesn't make us sinners. God knows we're not perfect. If you start taking everything literally, you're going to get yourself into trouble."

I was purposely working slowly, munching a tasteless piece of cold, leathery pizza, to waste time. I was hoping to engage him in a meaningful discussion so he'd realize I was right, and stop being such an aggravating religious zealot.

"God never said we could pick and choose what we wanted to believe. If you murder somebody, doesn't that make you a murderer? If you rob someone, you're a robber. If you tell a lie, you're a liar. It doesn't matter how many times you kill, rob, or lie. So if you sin, why aren't you a sinner? Mom, why do you go to confession if you're not a sinner?"

"That's ridiculous," I answered angrily. "Let's not compare me to a murderer or a robber." I could feel myself getting hot under the collar again. "Tell me, do you know anyone who's perfect?"

"Not a soul; not even you, Mom. I love you, you silver-haired, knuckleheaded old lady, but you're not perfect." David was very wisely trying to change the mood before it got out of hand again.

"Well, I'm practically perfect. Your father always says he married an angel. How much closer to perfection can you get?" I joked back. "Is my halo on straight?"

"Do you screw that thing on, Mom? I see a few ridges there on your forehead."

"Kill, Manfred, kill!" I said to the hungry dog who was happily helping us clean up the crumbs.

As I opened the front door to let Manfred out, I felt a playful push and found myself on the doorstep in my trusty pink furry slippers and fleecy robe, pink velcro rollers in my hair. The door was locked behind me.

"David, let me in before this dog starts barking and wakes up the neighborhood. I'm counting to ten and then I'll scream! One . . . two . . . three . . . "

"Who is it?" David asked in a sing-songy voice, still kidding around.

"It's Mary Poppins, practically perfect in every way. Now let me in or I'll huff and I'll puff and I'll blow this split level trap right down to the ground."

"Who did you say it was? I didn't hear you."

"*David Joseph Connelly*, you're grounded for the rest of your life!!! Four . . . five . . . six . . . seven."

"Okay, I'll let you in, but you have to say the password and there's no takebacks."

"Password, password . . ." I thought. "Pizza!"

"Wrong! Try again. I'll give you a hint; it has something to do with being not perfect."

Not perfect, not perfect, hmmm . . . sinner, that's it! . . . "I'm a sinner . . . sinner . . . sinner!" I yelled through megaphoned hands.

"Bingo!" David roared.

Manfred started barking ferociously as if to agree with me. (I could have sworn he yelped, "You got that right," in a quaint Irish setter brogue.)

The neighbor's window suddenly shot up. "Who's out there? Is that you, Laurette? Are you locked out? Is something wrong? Shall I send Charlie down?"

"No, no!" I said. "Don't do that! It's all right."

The front door quickly flew open and David whisked me in. "Are you trying to get us arrested for disturbing the peace? Sometimes I think you're into premature senility," David laughed.

John stood at the top of the steps in his wrinkled blue pajama bottoms with Liz and Peggy, our twenty-one-year-old twins. "What's all the racket?" they asked, rubbing the sleep from their eyes. "What were you doing outside? It's almost midnight!"

"Go back to bed. Everything's under control. I've just made an astounding announcement, that's all. We'll talk about it tomorrow."

"Keep it down, will you? I have an early meeting in the morning," Liz said as she dragged her weary little body back to bed. Peggy just shook her head like she wasn't sure if she was dreaming or not.

David and I collapsed on the sofa laughing. "You know I had my fingers crossed all the time, don't you?" I said.

"Absolutely no takebacks," he said, running up the stairs to his room. "And that's my final word."

As I lay in bed giggling at the silly juvenile fun we'd had, the tape in my mind was on replay. I thought about the proclamation I'd made. "I'm a sinner." I'd been denying it for a long time, but basically I knew David was right. I often sinned and that did make me a sinner.

*　　*　　*

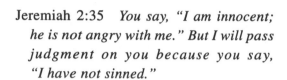

Psalm 143:2   *Do not bring your servant into judgment, for no one living is righteous before you.*

Jeremiah 2:35   *You say, "I am innocent; he is not angry with me." But I will pass judgment on you because you say, "I have not sinned."*

Romans 3:10   *As it is written: "There is no one righteous, not even one."*

Romans 3:23   *All have sinned and fall short of the glory of God.*

Romans 5:12   *Therefore, just as sin entered the world through one man, and death through sin, and in this way death came to all men, because all sinned . . .*

1 John 1:10   *If we claim we have not sinned, we make him out to be a liar and his word has no place in our lives.*

CHAPTER TWO

You can't get to heaven on filthy rags!

Somewhere along the line, Valerie, our twenty-four-year-old perennial student who had always had a mind of her own, began to follow closely in David's footsteps, sharing his excitement and enthusiasm. Valerie had attended a Christian weekend conference with a friend. Now she was voluntarily heading to church, sometimes twice on Sundays with a Bible under her arm.

Could this be the same girl who had been going in one door of the local cathedral to pick up a Sunday bulletin and continuing right out the other door? (Grab a bulletin, go out next door, do not pray, do not listen to the sermon, do not give money to the collection, do not receive Communion, do not pass go.) As the bulletins piled up week after week, we naturally figured she was a faithful attender. It never occurred to us that she had no idea what was going on at church. But that wasn't important. As long as she went for Sunday Mass, we asked nothing more from her. She was fulfilling her Sunday obligation (or at least we thought she was) for which we were grateful.

Now I had two of my children walking around behind me quoting Scripture. How long would this phase last? How long would I last? Having my religious beliefs undermined by my own children was stirring up a mixture of emotions that left my nerves raw and ready to pounce at the slightest provocation.

Just a week earlier Valerie had told me that my good works were like filthy rags! Filthy rags! All the years I'd tended the needs of kids, dogs, cats, gerbils, ducks, relatives, friends, and strangers, and all the years of teaching sixth grade CCD were no more than filthy rags? One year of sixth grade teaching ought to be enough to qualify me for sainthood. There was the hospital volunteer work and cooking for the priests. These things had to count for something. I was expecting thousands of gold stars beside my name in the heavenly ledger.

These two Bible-toting kids were wearing me thin. They claimed to have a personal relationship with God, but their relationship with me was on thin ice.

"Sure, you have a relationship with God," I scoffed. "And Saint Peter and I are distant cousins on my mother's side." If it wasn't so abrasive, it might even have been comical.

The latest question was, "Mom, do you know for sure that when you die, you'll go to heaven?"

"Excuse me, but my crystal ball is in the shop. Ask me again next week." Were they privy to some deep mystical after-life secret?

"I just want to be where your father is, so you'd better ask him where he plans to go. You know, 'wither thou goest, I will go' and all that. I think that's Shakespeare."

"No, it's not Shakespeare. That's what Ruth said to Naomi in the Bible." Valerie chuckled in a smart-alecky tone.

How about that? I was quoting Scripture and I didn't even know it. Maybe it was contagious.

"I knew that," I said very unconvincingly.

When my friend Jolee stopped in for coffee the next day, we got into the filthy rag idea. "Can you beat that?" I said. "All my good deeds, like filthy rags! What am I going to do with them?"

"Well, I don't know about the kids, but you can't get to heaven on filthy rags." We both picked up on the cue and simultaneously broke into a ridiculous song we'd known as kids. *Oh, you can't get to heaven . . . on filthy rags . . . 'cause the Lord don't allow no filthy rags there . . . No, you can't get to heaven on filthy rags . . . I ain't a gonna grieve my Lord no mo'."* Ha, ha! "Where did we resurrect that one from?"

We set our coffee cups down and shuffled out the door in step to our off-key singing, waving our hands in the air like spiritual Gospel singers, *"You can't get to heaven on filthy rags . . . I ain't a gonna grieve my Lord no mo'. . . "* We were meeting a crew to clean house for Mary, an elderly lady in need of serious help.

Mary's Early American cottage was all done up in chintz and chichi. It was nauseatingly feminine, and every bit of fluff and ruffle was thick with years of accumulated dust. The smoky gray crisscross Priscilla curtains revealed a window covered with nose prints from her blind German shepherd dog, Fifi. There was smelly litter and creepy crawly things in every little nook and cranny.

Eight of us worked feverishly for five hours without a break. Mary's little house was still dingy when we left. But the curtains and windows were clean. It was free of debris and smelled heavenly of disinfectant. (This had to be a four-star good deed. Hopefully it was enough to keep me out of purgatory for several months, if not forever.)

After we finished, I handed Jolee half the rags we'd used. "Here's your meager wages, Cinderella. You better put them in your safety deposit box. You may need to turn them in for a golden crown someday." Well, if nothing else, the whole rag idea had been good for a laugh.

I climbed into bed that evening with the rag song still humming in my mind, *"No, you can't get to heaven . . . on filthy rags . . . filthy rags . . . filthy rags."* Before I knew it, I was sound asleep and standing at the pearly gates of heaven in a tattered white gown and faded pink furry slippers, laboriously dragging a heavy, damp, overflowing pouch behind me.

"What have you got there?" Saint Peter asked in a powerful, reverberating voice.

"They're my good deeds, sir," I said, grunting, groaning, and heaving as I dragged my precious, hard-earned cargo an inch at a time. "I have a lot of them, eighty years' worth. You want to count them, your honor, sir? There must be thousands. . . . "

"They smell bad, like dirty, wet rags," he said. "The Lord don't allow no filthy rags in here. You'll have to take those down below. There's a flight of stairs over in the corner. Just keep going down . . . down . . . down . . . You'll know when you get there. You'll feel the heat and hear strange sounds, like gnashing of teeth."

"Oh but your highness, sir, this is so heavy. I can hardly move it . . . ugh . . . groan. I thought I could bring them up here. I thought this was my admission price."

"Where did you ever get that idea? And don't call me 'your highness,' we're all the same up here."

"Yes, sir . . . I mean, no sir . . . I mean . . . okay. Couldn't I just leave them out here someplace and come in?"

"No, no, they'd just be in the way; they're entirely useless. Besides they're *dirty, filthy . . . wet and smelly . . . wet and smelly . . . smelly . . . smelly . . . filthy . . . weeettt . . . smelllllly . . . "*

"Aaaaagh! No . . . I don't want to go down there! No . . . no . . . stop . . . don't push me . . . Stop pushing!!!!"

"Laurette, Laurette, wake up!" John was shaking me abruptly.

"Stop pushing! I don't want . . . I don't want . . . no, I don't!" I was sitting up in bed punching John with both fists.

"Laurette, stop it! You're having a bad dream, something about rags, smelly rags. Roll over honey, it's okay. Everything's fine."

Fine? Fine? No, it wasn't fine. My heart was beating like a bongo drum. My nightgown was soaked to the skin. I jumped into my pink furry slippers and hobbled downstairs to get a cold drink. "Whew! What a nightmare!" I thought. "These kids must be getting to me more than I want to admit."

As soon as I thought it was a respectable hour to call Jolee, I dialed her number. When I heard a very groggy "Helloooo," I knew my timing was poor. "I'm sorry, Jolee, did I wake you?"

14

"No, I had to get up to answer the phone anyway," she answered kiddingly, even at 7:45 a.m. "It better be important," she added between loud yawns.

"Well, I think it is. I had such a nightmare last night, I couldn't get back to sleep. I've been up since three-thirty . . . "

"You could have called me then; I was still up. What's on your mind?" she asked patiently.

"Remember when we spoke about finding a Bible study?"

"You woke me up to talk about Bible study? . . . Good night."

"No, Jolee, wait. If I find one, will you go with me?"

"I will if you let me go back to sleep now."

"Thanks, Jolee. I'll call you later."

"Much later," she said facetiously, leaving me alone with a lonely dial tone.

At 9:01 I started making phone calls. "Good morning, Saint Joseph's rectory. May I help you?" chimed a very sweet lady's voice.

"I'm looking to find a Bible study. I wonder if you know of one either here or at one of the other parishes around?"

"No, I'm sorry. I don't know of a Bible study anywhere around. We do have regular catechism classes and classes in doctrine and theology. Would you be interested in one of those?"

"Good morning, Saint Paul's rectory, Father Mike *heah*." . . . This time it was a strong man's voice with a pronounced New England accent.

"Can you tell me where I could go for Bible study? I can't seem to find one locally. I wondered if you have classes at any time."

"No, we don't have Bible study *heah*, but we do have catechism classes for adults, every now and then. Would that interest you?"

"Good morning, Saint Anthony's . . . No, we don't have Bible study. We have novenas every Monday evening."

"Saint Luke's, Sister Saint Marcelle speaking . . . Bible study? Oh no! We have nothing like that."

"Like what?" I thought. "Did I say something sinful?"

15

No! . . . No! . . . No! Came one response after another. I could have classes in church tradition, church doctrine, and church history, but a Bible study seemed to be an impossible request. There was only one thing to do. I'd have to try other denominations.

"Good morning, Church of the Rock. May I help you? . . . Yes, we have a weekly Bible study. Are you a member of our church? . . . No? Oh, I'm sorry, but our study is only for our church ladies. Perhaps you'd like to become a member."

"I don't think so," I answered crisply. ("I'd as soon join the Ku Klux Klan," I thought to myself.)

So far my search for Bible knowledge was going nowhere and I was getting discouraged. In my desperation, I decided to try the church Valerie and David had been attending. They didn't have to know about it.

"Chapel on the Square, good morning . . . yes, we have a Bible study every Monday evening or Tuesday morning. We'd love to have you join us."

"Voilà!" Success, at last. I began to dial Jolee's number with a strange excitement. Why was I so thrilled? All I wanted to do was prove the kids wrong.

"Hi, Jolee, are you free Monday night? We just need to bring a Bible and show up. Are you game?"

"I'm game to try it once, but I'm not making any commitment."

The following Monday evening we set out with Bible in hand. I put mine in a large canvas tote bag so no one would notice. We arrived at this strange-looking church with not a stained glass window in sight. I couldn't smell candles or incense. There were no statues, not even an altar. It didn't look like a church to me. We were directed to a room where a group of about thirty women of all ages sat at round tables sipping decaf coffee and nibbling chocolate chip cookies. The women were quick to notice us and one of them invited us to join her table. They all had small tattered-looking Bibles. "Wouldn't you think they could afford to buy new ones?" I thought.

When I opened up the huge family-sized Bible that I'd received for a wedding gift, it took up half the table. The leader, Mrs. Frank, a tall, attractive silver-haired lady with a twinkle in her eye, greeted us warmly. "We're so glad you've joined us tonight," she said as she introduced us to the rest of the group. "This semester we're studying the books of Titus and Philemon. We're up to chapter three in the book of Titus. Don't hesitate to ask questions as we move along."

The books of Titus and who? I hadn't brought any other book, only the Bible, and I was already confused. Mrs. Frank took one look at my oversized Bible and suggested it might be easier for me to use one of their pew Bibles.

She handed me a small gray, hardcover Bible and said graciously, "Page 1108." Jolee shot a bewildered, nervous glance my way as she fumbled noisily through the pages of her brand new paperback "New Testament" Bible.

"Page 1108," I whispered, trying to help her out.

"I only have 400 pages," she answered curtly.

A few people started to giggle, but the discreet leader quickly picked up another pew Bible. "Page 1108," she said gently as she handed the book to a very flustered Jolee. By now there was no question in anyone's mind that we were as Bible illiterate as could be.

"Paul is the author of the book of Titus," Mrs. Frank said for our benefit, "and we're in chapter three. We'll read verses three through five and then discuss them before going further."

Verses 1-2, *"Remind the people to be subject to rulers and authorities, to be obedient, to be ready to do whatever is good, to slander no one, to be peaceable and considerate, and to show true humility toward all men."*

(So far it sounded pretty good. Be a good person. I had no argument with that. That's what I'd said all along. This was going to be easier than I thought.)

Verse 3, *"At one time we too were foolish, disobedient, deceived, and enslaved by all kinds of passions and pleasures. We lived in malice and envy, being hated and hating one another."*

(Wow, what kind of people were they? I'm glad I'm not anything like that.)

Verses 4-5, *"But when the kindness and love of God our Savior appeared, he saved us, not because of righteous things we had done, but because of his mercy. He saved us through the washing of rebirth and renewal by the Holy Spirit."*

(Oh, oh, this sounds familiar. I don't think I like this.)

My hand shot up. "Excuse me, but what do you mean 'not by works of righteousness which we have done'? Are you saying that our good deeds don't count?"

"Well, *I'm* not really saying anything. I'm reading the Word of God. But this verse is saying that we're not saved on the basis of the good things we do, but only by God's grace. The simplest and clearest truth of the Gospel is that people don't go to heaven because they're good. The way to heaven is through Jesus Christ," Mrs. Frank explained kindly but with solid conviction, as she looked at my foggy expression above the half moon glasses that sat on the tip of her thin nose.

Everyone sat there nodding their heads in agreement. I heard an undertone voice saying, "Wow, that's soooo great!"

"Great? What's so great?" I thought. "If I can't get to heaven by being good, then I've wasted a lot of my time." It didn't sound right to me. Were these women pulling my leg or did they really understand and believe this stuff?

Jolee looked from Mrs. Frank to me and shook her head in disagreement. "I believe in Jesus Christ, " she said, "but I think you have to do good things also. You're saying all I have to do is believe? That just sounds too simple."

"Well, it is simple for us. So simple that we keep trying to add to it. But it wasn't simple for Christ; it cost him his life. Let's look at a couple of other verses and see if we can clarify this point for you. Vickie, would you read Ephesians 2:8-9? . . . Page 1083," she added as she saw Jolee and me floundering.

Vickie looked more like a movie star than a Scripture scholar. Everything on her body was still firm enough to jog in public. She had a habit of running her fingers through her long strawberry blonde hair in a very glamorous way. Vickie flipped to the right passage without skipping a beat and began to read with an angelic voice. *"'For it is by grace you have been saved, through faith—and this not from yourselves, it is the gift of God—not by works, so that no one can boast.'"*

"You see, your good works don't earn your salvation. They're a result of your salvation. Salvation is a gift, not a reward," Mrs. Frank explained. "Betsy, will you read Galatians 2:21?"

"'I do not set aside the grace of God, for if righteousness could be gained through the law, Christ died for nothing,'" Betsy read.

"If we could get to heaven by being good, then Christ died for nothing," explained Mrs. Frank. "We could never be good enough. We're told, *'Be ye holy because I am holy.'* God's goal for his children is perfection. That's why we can't get there on our own. There's none perfect, not one. Ginny, will you read Isaiah 64:6?"

Ginny adjusted her very thick spectacles, cleared her throat nervously, and read from her large print Bible. They all seemed to know exactly where to find things in this maze of words. *"'All of us have become like one who is unclean, and all our righteous acts are like filthy rags; we all shrivel up like a leaf, and like the wind our sins sweep us away.'"*

Filthy rags!! There it was in black and white. The kids were right. It was in the Bible. I was beginning to feel a little sick. In the stillness that followed, I heard myself heaving a heavy sigh.

Mrs. Frank's voice broke the silence. Her tone became gentle and motherly as if she was speaking to a confused child. "You see, it really doesn't matter what we consider to be good works. If you live to be a hundred you could never earn heaven; it's a free gift. Our good deeds are wonderful for society, of course. But they're not acceptable to God until we've come to Christ. We have to be cleansed of our sin first. It's the cleansing that makes us and our gifts acceptable. Until you're cleansed, your good works are like filthy rags. You simply can't get to heaven on your good works."

19

Jolee and I tried to muffle a chuckle, remembering our giddiness from the previous week, *"Oh you can't get to heaven on your good works . . . 'cause the Lord don't allow no good works there . . . I ain't a gonna grieve my Lord no mo'."*

"I'm sorry; it's just a silly private joke," I said, feeling a little flushed.

I was getting fidgety. Wasn't it time to go home yet? I looked at my watch. It was only eight o'clock. Another half hour to go. What would I have to deal with next? I needed time to sift through this new information.

Mrs. Frank could just as readily have spent the next half hour reading Mother Goose nursery rhymes or reciting the Declaration of Independence. It wouldn't have mattered. All I could hear was, "You can't get to heaven on your good works."

When eight thirty came, the movie star closed in prayer. Mrs. Frank invited us to return the following week and not hesitate to call her at home if we had any questions.

Jolee and I quickly gathered up our belongings and left the church in a fierce lightning storm. Rain was coming down in sheets. The wind was howling. Tree limbs bowed down to the ground and branches littered the streets. If God was trying to speak to us, he was doing so with a mighty roar. "What do you think?" Jolee asked. "Are you ready for more of the same next week?"

"My first inclination is to say no." Just then a ferocious clap of thunder sent us both clinging to each other in a holy huddle. "But maybe I ought to reconsider," I added meekly. "I guess I'd rather God gave me heaven as a free gift than having to earn it myself. I've never been sure of how many good things God would consider enough. Do I need so many good deeds per year of my life? Do some deeds earn more points than others?"

"I know what you mean," Jolee said. "If we're on a point system, we ought to have a program of points earned, sort of like the frequent flyer method."

"Yeah, at the end of the year you should get a summary statement saying how many points you've earned for the year, and your grand total for your lifetime."

"Shouldn't it tell you how many more points you need so when you're getting close you can relax?" Jolee continued.

Jolee and I were so busy chuckling over our nonsense, we didn't see the unexpected huge puddle of water in the road. Fountains of rainwater shot over the roof of my little car and sent us swerving uncontrollably for just a few seconds before we stopped on the side of the road.

"Whoa!" I said straightening up the car. "Thank God there was no one else on the road."

"Yeah, we might have run out of point-collecting time sooner than we'd like," Jolee said only half kiddingly.

So far, it seemed like the kids were two for two. I really am a sinner and maybe I can't get to heaven on my good works.

*   *   *

Matthew 20:28   *"The Son of Man did not come to be served, but to serve, and to give his life as a ransom for many."*

John 14:6   *Jesus answered, "I am the way and the truth and the life. No one comes to the Father except through me."*

Acts 13:39   *Through him everyone who believes is justified from everything you could not be justified from by the law of Moses.*

Romans 3:20   *Therefore no one will be declared righteous in his sight by observing the law; rather, through the law we become conscious of sin.*

Galatians 2:21   *I do not set aside the grace of God, for if righteousness could be gained through the law, Christ died for nothing!*

Galatians 3:24   *So the law was put in charge to lead us to Christ that we might be justified by faith.*

Ephesians 2:8,9   *For it is by grace you have been saved, through faith—and this not from yourselves, it is the gift of God—not by works, so that no one can boast.*

2 Timothy 1:9   *Who has saved us and called us to a holy life—not because of anything we have done but because of his own purpose and grace. This grace was given us in Christ Jesus before the beginning of time.*

Titus 3:4-5   *But when the kindness and love of God our Savior appeared, he saved us, not because of righteous things we had done, but because of his mercy.*

Hebrews 11:6   *And without faith it is impossible to please God, because anyone who comes to him must believe that he exists and that he rewards those who earnestly seek him.*

Chapter Three

I'll wait for the movie.

For whatever reason, Jolee and I never went back to that study. Mrs. Frank called a couple of times, but we made one excuse after another until she finally got the message and gave up on us. We believed and accepted the things we'd heard, but we were afraid of what we'd hear next. It seemed safer and wiser to stay away. When it came to spiritual discussions, we were about as secure as a tiny, lone mouse who'd made a wrong turn onto "cat alley."

"Mom, you know what our pastor was speaking about this morning?" Valerie asked one Sunday when it seemed to me she'd spent the entire weekend at church. (What in the world did they find to do there all that time?)

"Don't tell me, let me guess," I said sarcastically. "Did it have anything to do with money or hell?"

"Neither," Valerie answered calmly. "He was speaking about the Word of God and how we got the Bible. It was fascinating. I'll get you the tape. I think you'd enjoy listening to it."

"Really? I know how I got my Bible. It was a wedding gift from Aunt Minnie's alcoholic, live-in boyfriend. He wrote in it, 'May you always find comfort in the pages of this book.' He'd found a lot of comfort, mostly Southern style, and it came in a bottle."

Valerie was looking at me as if she couldn't believe what she was hearing. "I guess you don't want to hear about it," she mumbled picking up her stack of Christian paraphernalia and heading up

23

the stairs. She was acquiring quite a library of tracts, books, and tapes.

My knitting needles were clicking away at breakneck speed, but I'd lost all track of my knitting and pearling again. I was making a yellow coat for the dog which originally started out as a baby sweater for a friend. But I'd gotten mixed up so often that I'd ended up with three armholes. Now, I wasn't sure whether I had an extra armhole or I was short one. In any case it would keep my faithful pet warm this winter. Manfred was snuggled cozily at my feet, resting his head on my pink furry slippers without a care in the world. Now and then he woke up and attacked the ball of yellow yarn with a mad vengeance.

"Manfred, I'm making this for you. You're going to love it. Trust me. When the cold weather comes, you'll be glad to wear this." But the look on his face seemed to betray his faithfulness, and I knew what he was thinking, *"Grrr . . . in your dreams. You'll never get that thing on me . . . grrr . . . I have my pride. Find yourself a three-legged mongrel who has no fashion sense."* Even the animals had a mind of their own. The nunnery was looking more and more inviting all the time.

I felt relieved when I heard Valerie's bedroom door close. I'd won the battle by not allowing her to get me involved in yet another exasperating spiritual discussion. Still somehow I felt I was the loser in this situation. I surely had a curiosity about the Bible, but I was afraid of giving the children an inch. If they were on an assignment to convert me, they were going to meet with more than a bit of resistance. I was not about to make it easy for them.

John had taken the boys out to a pre-season football game. Liz and Peggy were out cruising the mall with friends. Lydia was seldom around since she had her own apartment. Valerie and I were alone in the house, but we were two floors apart. What a waste of precious time. It wasn't long before I realized how foolish I'd been. Valerie had wanted to talk about something she considered of value. I'd blown it. Brick by brick, I was building a wall to rival the famous one in China that can even be seen from outer space. Why was I so defensive? What was at the root of my behavior? Was it pride? Insecurity? Both? Hmmm—possibly.

Shouldn't I be encouraging the fact that she was excited about a sermon? If she'd asked me what I'd heard at church that morning, I would have been hard pressed to tell her. It was long gone. All I remembered was that I'd gotten into the wrong pew on my way back from receiving Communion. I didn't realize my mistake till I took the hand of the man beside me and found I had the wrong husband. His grumpy-looking wife shot an accusing glance my way as if to say: "Let go of my husband, you hussy. And in church too, tsk . . . tsk . . . have you no shame?"

John tried to smother his hysterical giggling behind me. I knew he'd lost control when he faked choking and walked out during the closing hymn while everyone was fumbling around for their purses and umbrellas. No one seemed to have much interest in singing except for one solitary woman in the back who had a beautiful and loud soprano voice. She was very willingly doing an unexpected solo. *"Faith of our Fathers, living still. In spite of dungeon, fire, and sword! . . . We will be true to thee till death."*

Valerie's experience with church seemed a bit more significant than mine. When I got up enough courage to go upstairs, I knocked on Valerie's door. She was getting ready to go out again and was not overly exuberant at my appearance.

"I'm sorry I was so flippant, Valerie. I really would like to hear what your pastor had to say this morning. Sometimes I just have trouble dealing with the fact that you've left our church. I don't understand why you felt that was necessary and I react negatively."

"I'll get you the tape," she said as she slipped on a pretty pink, dotted Swiss dress with a frilly white collar. There was such a chill in her voice, I could almost see her breath.

I looked at her white sandals. "Want to borrow my pink slippers? They're a perfect match for your dress." I was clearly trying to make amends.

"No thanks, I wouldn't want to traumatize you. You might pin them to my socks so I wouldn't lose them, like you did with my mittens till I was fourteen. But you could let me borrow your pink ceramic necklace and earrings. I think that would help."

There seemed to be a little string attached to reconciliation.

"If you get me the tape, I'll listen to it. I don't promise to agree with what I hear, but I will listen," I said, slipping the necklace over her long silky dark hair. "That dress looks great on you. You look like a princess."

"Thanks, Mom. I'll be home late. A group of us are going to the Light Club after the concert tonight."

"The Light Club?"

"Yes, it's like a night club except they play Christian music. They only serve soft drinks and there's no smoking. It's a Christian place."

Now I'd heard everything. A Christian night club!

Val grabbed her Bible and ran down the stairs happy as a lark. "Got to run. I'm late. I'll see about the tape. Maybe sometime you'll come to a concert with me. You really would enjoy it . . . *bye.*"

Oh, there it was . . . I gave her an inch and she assumed I meant to give her a foot. Do mothers ever win?

Without fail, I was presented with two tapes the following Sunday. "I got one for Jolee too. Let me know how you like it."

Every night for the next two weeks Valerie asked, "Did you get a chance to listen to the tape yet? Did you give Jolee hers?"

"No, to both!" I finally bellowed in exasperation. "I'll get to it. Get off my case!"

Valerie was visibly disappointed but nonetheless diligent. "Okay, but I don't know what you're afraid of. After all, I'm not trying to get you to listen to the teachings of Sun Myung Moon. We're talking about the Bible here."

David and Matt were having a friendly wrestling match on the living room floor. David had Matt pinned and was starting the count-down when Matt flipped over and jumped up with a shout of triumph.

"Now I'm taking out the big guns. Say your prayers; it's all over."

"Maybe I'd better say my prayers; I think I've been dodging the big guns for months," I mumbled incoherently under my breath. John was laughing with the guys, cheering them on, "Go get him, Matt, grab his legs! Don't let him get away from you." He was totally oblivious to the heated exchange between Valerie and me.

I felt like my shoulders were being pinned to the floor and I was hearing the countdown. *One . . . Two . . . Three.* I could almost visualize the pitiful saga. Valerie, wearing a skimpy, shiny green uniform, stood with an evil grin on her face, one foot poised smugly on my buttocks, her hair dripping wet. The referee was holding her right arm up in the air triumphantly. "The winner! Valerie Connelly at 105 lbs. scores an unprecedented victory over an opponent of considerably higher weight and lower intelligence, wearing an outdated uniform and dirty worn-out pink furry slippers!"

Valerie proudly took her bows while the crowd broke into wild cheering and applause.

"Val . . . rrreee . . . Val . . . rreee . . . Val . . . reee!!" They chanted. In the meantime, her tired old invalid mother lay in a crumpled heap on the floor, the flagrant victim of parent abuse by a violent child.

John jolted me back to reality with an affectionate tug on my long pony tail and a peck on the cheek. "Penny for your thoughts, Mom. Hey, it's five o'clock. Cocktail time, isn't it?" Oh, how I enjoyed the intimacy in the tender touches and hugs we shared. We had a number of rough spots in our marriage, but our relationship had never been dull. We were still in love after almost thirty years together.

A few days later Jolee and I drove two hours to the Jersey Shore to visit her mother. We'd packed a picnic lunch and planned to spend a few glorious hours on the beach, relaxing in the sun. If we listened to the tape on the way, maybe I could get Valerie to stop nagging me.

We popped the tape in and heard a heavenly choir singing . . . *"Jesus is coming to earth again; What if it were today? Coming in love and power to reign; What if it were today? Glory . . . Glory . . . joy to my heart it will bring: Glory . . . Glory!"*

"That's a loaded question, isn't it?" Jolee suggested. "What if it were today? I'm not sure I'd be ready to meet my Maker. How about you?"

It was a loaded question, one that I'd been asked many times in the past year. The answer was something I preferred not to think about.

As soon as the last strains of the hymn were over, a man's gentle but commanding voice began to pray and then speak, "Most people who say they don't believe the Bible have never read the Bible." (That was an interesting opening statement. He was probably right.)

"People often ask, "How can I know the Bible is true? How is the Bible relevant in today's society? Can I trust the Bible to be accurate? Is it really God's Word?' If you're struggling with any of these questions, I'm not sure I can answer them all in forty minutes. But if your mind and heart are open to God's teaching, you'll hear all that you need to hear."

While I drove, Jolee sat with pen in hand ready to jot down any questions or disagreements we might have.

"The Bible is not like any other book you have on the shelf. It's a living book. It was written by men, but inspired by God."

"In the Old Testament, God predicted a multitude of events to happen in the future. They've come true exactly as predicted, even to the minutest detail."

Jolee would rewind the tape periodically to catch something she'd missed. "This really is fascinating," she acknowledged as she hastily wrote between sips of hot coffee. She already had three pages of information. "Do you have any questions or disagreements yet?"

"I don't know enough to disagree or to ask questions. I'm one of the people he spoke about who never believed the Bible but

I've never read it," I admitted. "It's going to take more than one man's sermon to convince me that it should be taken literally."

The pastor went on to discuss the evidence for the Resurrection, according to history professors, theologians, and lawyers who had done extensive studies on the subject. He told of the eye witnesses and the twelve cowardly men who bravely went on to die martyrs' deaths after they'd seen the risen Christ.

For the next thirty minutes we heard this man expound and present amazing proof for the authenticity of Scripture. Jolee and I were mesmerized.

"With all of the evidence to support the Word of God, are you still turning a deaf ear to him? Listen to what James, the brother of Jesus, writes in his epistle. James 1:21, *'Therefore, get rid of all moral filth and the evil that is so prevalent, and humbly accept the word planted in you, which can save you.'*

"If you want to know God, there's only one place to look, that's in his Word. That's where he reveals himself to us."

Jolee's ears and mine perked up at that. . . . "He will reveal himself to us? . . . Brother of Jesus? What brother? Question number one."

"We'll ask my mother," Jolee offered. "She'll know. She's been going to a Bible study for over a year now. She'd love nothing better than to hear me ask questions about the Bible. She's been praying for me for years."

Jolee's mom was waiting outside her yellow mobile home when we arrived. Several of her white-haired neighbors sat on their front lawns, straining their eyes to carefully scrutinize every car that pulled into their homey little senior citizen park. When they spotted Jolee, one after another waved approvingly.

"Hi, Jo, your mom's been waiting for you," one of them shouted loud enough to drown out the roar of incoming planes. "Save us some of that pie she made. We could smell it baking all morning."

"Hi, Mrs. Reith. I'll be sure to save a big piece especially for you," replied Jolee fondly.

29

Mrs. Reith leaned over to her companions with a perplexed look. "What did she say?"

"She said it's special having such a nice view," reported one of the residents blessed with better hearing.

"Oh, what a nice girl!" said Mrs. Reith.

Wilma was a wispy little lady in her mid to late seventies. She had a coquettish look about her. Her deep dimples and head full of curls gave her the appearance of an aging Shirley Temple. I half expected to hear the tap, tap, tapping of Mary Jane shoes as she walked. She welcomed us with warm hugs and homemade blueberry pie. Her small humble trailer was tidy and cozy with pretty flower boxes filled with red geraniums and hanging ivy. The smell of fresh baking permeated the air. One entire wall was covered with treasured family photos of Jolee, her sisters, and all the grandchildren. Beside her rocking chair sat a well-worn red leather Bible with all sorts of bookmarks sticking out of the gold-edged pages.

"Mom, I need to ask you a Biblical question. Do you know if Jesus had any brothers? I always thought he was an only child, but Laurette and I were listening to a tape on the way over here. This man said Jesus had a brother named James. Is that right?"

"Oh yes, that's right. In fact, he had quite a few brothers and sisters. I'll show you in the book of Matthew." She opened up to Matthew 13:55 and read, *"'Isn't this the carpenter's son? Isn't his mother's name Mary, and aren't his brothers James, Joseph, Simon, and Judas? Aren't all his sisters with us?'"*

"Wow!" I said. "Why didn't we know that? I thought Mary was always a virgin. Isn't that what we were taught?"

"Uh-huh," said Wilma, "but the Bible clearly states that she was a virgin until she gave birth to her firstborn son."

"Oh, well, that's news to me."

Seizing the opportunity, Wilma grabbed her Bible and her portable tape player as we went out the door for a day on the beach. "I'd like to listen to that tape," she said.

We spent several hours sitting in the hot sun under a large striped umbrella, admiring the beauty of the ocean with its crashing waves, watching the noisy seagulls diving gracefully at the smell of food. Children were running in and out of the surf with loud squeals of laughter. Others were building elaborate sand castles with moats around them to keep invaders from attacking. A steady flow of young girls clad in scanty bikinis paraded before the handsome, golden tan lifeguards who sat on high stools pridefully flexing their youthful muscles.

"Why don't they flex those muscles when we walk by?" Jolee asked playfully. "You think it's our bathing suits?"

"I don't know. Your green iridescent water shoes give you a certain pizazz," I laughed, "but I could probably use a new swim suit."

"What's wrong with the one you're wearing? If you mend the hole in the knee, it may last a few more years."

"I'll have you know this is an official 'Miss America' suit."

"Really? What year was that . . . 1928?" Jolee asked as she struggled to open her sand chair.

"I hope you sit on a bad tempered, giant crab."

In no time, Jolee was fully engrossed in one of Danielle Steele's steamy novels. Her mom, Wilma, was rotating between the tape player and the Bible. Earphones sat precariously on her head so as not to disturb the cutesy curls, and kept us from hearing a sound. She was frantically highlighting passages and making occasional exclamatory sounds. "Oh wow! . . . That's right . . . Amen! . . . Absolutely!"

Jolee, preoccupied with her alluring book, would only let out a little snicker or a giggle every so often. I was deliberately trying to ignore both of them and allowing my mind to be filled with nothing but air. I had come here to relax; that's what I planned to do. But my companions were bent on disturbing my peace by sharing literary gems of one sort or another.

"Listen to this, Laurette," and then would come a quote either from Danielle Steele or from Moses. Both Jolee and Wilma were convinced that I would remain in ignorant bliss unless I heard the wisdom expounded by one of these authors. One of them was wrong!

When it was time to enjoy our picnic lunch, there was no keeping Wilma quiet. She was on a spiritual high. We were on her turf now. She'd made all kinds of notes and was comparing them with the notes Jolee had taken. Wilma confirmed much of what we'd heard on the tape by verifying it with appropriate Scripture. She was determined to squeeze as much information as she could into us while we were a captive audience.

I could feel myself bristling. My spirit was beginning to resist all input. Afraid that I might say something offensive, I started to pack things up. The picnic was over. I could sense the disappointment in Wilma's voice. "I have a book I'd like to loan you," she said. "It's called *A Ready Defense* by Josh McDowell. It's like a mini encyclopedia. I found it to be very helpful. I still refer to it all the time."

I wasn't sure I wanted any more questions answered for a while. I felt like a giant tidal wave had been hovering over me for months. Now the menacing wave was about to break and drag me out to sea.

"Enough!" . . . I wanted to scream . . . "Back off! . . . You're coming a little too close." I bit my tongue till I could almost taste the blood, and said nothing. But my body language must have spoken volumes. Poor Wilma looked a bit like a dejected puppy.

Reading the Bible had never been encouraged when I was growing up. At least not for lay people. Only the clergy had the training and wisdom to interpret God's Word. But now I was hearing that it was everyone's privilege and responsibility to study what the Bible had to say. It was more than a little scary to me. I'd rather munch popcorn and watch Charlton Heston in the movie version.

Nevertheless, Jolee and I listened to the tape again on the way home, rewinding it frequently to hear a specific portion. Though we were both a little intimidated, still we were like a couple of rebellious kids exploring forbidden territory, and savoring every curious but delicious discovery.

After listening, we drove the rest of the way home in relative silence. I was surprised at the thoughts floating around in my head.

("The kids have found something I surely don't have . . . I'd love to attend a service at Valerie's church sometime and see the pastor . . . Maybe I could make an appointment to talk to him . . . I know that wouldn't set right with John. Could I risk making waves at home?") Maybe the thing to do was to talk to the pastor at my own church first. That seemed a safer alternative for keeping peace in the family.

Many of the things I was hearing were not new to me. I'd heard some of them most of my growing-up years. I had no doubt in my mind that Jesus was Messiah. He was the Savior, the Son of God, and he was God. I had a lot of undeniable facts, but interwoven between facts was a lot of tradition and fiction that I was finding had no Biblical support. How was I to sort through fact and fiction? Whom could I believe? Was the answer to be found in the teachings of a church? Who could say which church was right? Surely the God of love didn't mean for us to live in a state of confusion about his truth. That truth had to be within the grasp of every single human being. At this point (though I would have been very reticent to admit it to anyone yet), I was determined to find that truth. My goal of proving the children wrong had dramatically backfired.

The words I'd heard the pastor speak on the tape came back to mind: *With all the evidence to support the Word of God, are you still turning a deaf ear to him? . . . If your heart and mind are open, you'll hear all you need to hear . . . God reveals himself in his Word.* Was that really possible? Would I find truth in his Word? I heard my own voice breaking through my thoughts, "Truth, that's where it's at, the truth!"

Jolee gave me an inquisitive look, "Bruce, my neighbor, tells me that truth is whatever one perceives it to be."

"Well, that's convenient. Then Bruce can believe anything he wants to believe and call it truth."

"He doesn't believe the holocaust really happened."

"Hmmm, I rest my case! Believing a lie doesn't make it true. I could perceive that I have a Barbie-doll figure, but you and I both know that's not truth."

"Oh, we do, yes we do! That is so untrue!" Jolee affirmed nodding her head persistently. "No question about that. That would be such deception! That would be a humongous lie."

"All right, all right! . . . Give me a break! A simple un-huh would be sufficient."

Jolee was carrying on like this was the biggest joke she'd ever heard. She was holding her sides and wiping the laughing tears from her eyes till the book on her lap went sliding down to the floor.

"Sometimes, Jo, you really tick me off!"

"Ouch!" she squealed, as she bent down to retrieve her book and banged her head on the dashboard with a loud thud.

"Oh . . . right now, I could become a believer," I said with a playful vengeance. "How sweet it is . . . Are you okay?"

"I'm fine," Jolee chuckled.

We both smiled, silently acknowledging the fact that our friendship was a rarity. We could tease and laugh at each other unmercifully. Yet we could also be very serious and protective when we had to be.

"I'm anxious to browse through this," Jolee said fingering the pages of her mom's book, "I have to admit I'm absolutely ignorant about the Bible and I'd like to know more. Who knows, maybe I'll become a true believer yet."

I made no comment, but I'd discreetly made a mental note of the book's interesting title: *A Ready Defense*.

Psalm 119:105   *Your word is a lamp to my feet and a light for my path.*

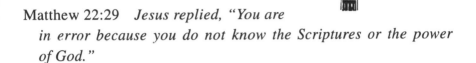

Jeremiah 22:29   *O land, land, land, hear the word of the Lord!*

Matthew 22:29   *Jesus replied, "You are in error because you do not know the Scriptures or the power of God."*

Luke 8:21   *He replied, "My mother and brothers are those who hear God's word and put it into practice."*

John 1:1   *In the beginning was the Word, and the Word was with God, and the Word was God.*

John 5:24   *"I tell you the truth, whoever hears my word and believes him who sent me has eternal life and will not be condemned; he has crossed over from death to life."*

John 8:31, 32   *To the Jews who had believed him, Jesus said, "If you hold to my teaching, you are really my disciples. Then you will know the truth, and the truth will set you free."*

Romans 10:17   *Consequently, faith comes from hearing the message, and the message is heard through the word of Christ.*

Colossians 3:16   *Let the word of Christ dwell in you richly as you teach and admonish one another with all wisdom, and as you sing psalms, hymns and spiritual songs with gratitude in your hearts to God.*

2 Timothy 3:16, 17   *All Scripture is God-breathed and is useful for teaching, rebuking, correcting and training in righteousness, so that the man of God may be thoroughly equipped for every good work.*

Hebrews 4:12   *For the word of God is living and active. Sharper than any double-edged sword, it penetrates even to dividing soul and spirit, joints and marrow; it judges the thoughts and attitudes of the heart.*

Matthew 1:25   *But he had no union with her until she gave birth to a son. And he gave him the name Jesus.*

CHAPTER FOUR

Is this a one-way street?

After everyone had left for the day, I was just about to settle down with a hot cup of coffee and cold cereal to enjoy my daily newspaper, when the phone rang. I figured whoever it was could talk to my answering machine. I planned to savor a lazy breakfast. I heard my own voice give its usual dull message: "I'm sorry there's no one home right now, but if you leave your name and phone number, we'll be sure to call you as soon as we return. Thank you for calling." . . . beep . . . beep . . . beep.

"Laurette, pick up the phone. I know you're home. You can drink your coffee and have breakfast while we chat." It was Jolee. This woman knew me dangerously well. It was a bit spooky.

"I suppose if I didn't answer the phone you'd drive over here. How did you know I was home?"

"Because I'm sitting in your driveway calling from my car phone. I can see you at the kitchen table. I brought my own coffee and I have two jelly doughnuts fresh from the bakery. If you don't let me in, I'll sit here and eat them by myself. Then you can watch me and salivate."

I opened the curtains and there was Jolee waving at me with a mischievous grin on her face. She was holding a familiar little white bag from the best bakery in town. This was the most unpredictable woman I'd ever met. If she was rich, she'd be called eccentric, but in reality, she was just strange.

37

"That's bribery!" I said, "but come on in. If you eat both those doughnuts, they'll settle on your hips before you get home. I can't let you do that. You're my friend." I was still speaking when the doorbell rang seven times without a break.

"Ding . . . dong . . . ding . . . dong . . . ding . . . dong . . . "

"Come on in, it's open!!!" I yelled. "Stop leaning on the bell. You sound like a pushy Avon lady!"

"Hi, friend. Hey, I've already done my laundry and marketing and you're not even dressed yet?" Jolee said, running her fingers wildly through my already messy hair.

"How many times have I asked you not to tousle my hair? I hate when you do that!"

"I don't know. A gazzillion?"

"More, much more."

"I can't help it. You're a teddy bear waiting to be tousled . . . You won't believe who I ran into at the supermarket . . . When are you going to get rid of those crazy pink furry slippers?"

"You expect Miss Universe? It's eight thirty in the morning. I brushed my teeth; what more do you want? . . . You're probably right. I wouldn't believe who you ran into, but tell me anyway."

"Remember Mrs. Frank, the Bible teacher at the Chapel on the Square? I was getting ice cream from the deep freezer and she was across the counter, but she didn't see me or recognize me."

"Sure, I remember her. Why does it surprise you to find her in the supermarket? The lady lives in the area. She has to shop somewhere."

"I know, but that's not all; she was talking to your friend Betty, the tall gal who lives in the big house over on Knob Hill." Jolee was setting the table as she was rambling on. "Oooh, pink napkins to match your pink slippers? How very elegant."

"So? They go to the same church. I still don't get why you're so wound up."

"You will. Guess who they were talking about."

"I don't know. The lunatic stalking them in frozen foods?"

"No, another lunatic. They were talking about you." Jolee was licking the jelly off her fingers.

"Me? Why me? Did you hear what they were saying?" Now my curiosity was aroused.

"Not all of it, but I did hear Mrs. Frank say she didn't know why you didn't come back for Bible study since you seemed to have a real interest. Then she included me . . . she said she didn't think either one of us had any understanding of the Bible."

"Why the nerve of them! What else did they say?"

"Then Betty said she was praying for you and she knew that it was just a matter of time before you discovered the truth. She said she was going to invite you for lunch sometime. Mrs. Frank said she would come too, so be prepared."

"Another one praying for me? What am I, a mass murderer? Well, I'm glad you warned me. Did they say anything else?"

"Yeah, Betty said she didn't think you knew that Jesus was the only way. And that's all I heard before someone else interrupted their conversation. What do you make of all that?"

"Hmmm . . . they must be missionaries in disguise and they think we're uncivilized pagans who need to be converted. They're right, I do have trouble with Jesus being the only way. I can't reconcile sweeping condemnation of outsiders with the loving teachings of Jesus . . . It doesn't seem fair. Did you buy only two doughnuts?"

"I wasn't planning a smorgasbord! Of course, I bought only two doughnuts! . . . I'm with you, that just doesn't sound right to me. I heard a woman on Oprah Winfrey the other day saying that there are many paths to God and that a loving God will draw all people to himself."

"I saw that show," I said. "I should have taped it as ammunition for the kids. I think I can accept that we're not saved by our good deeds, but it's very confusing. Lots of people are genuinely good wholesome people. They're compassionate, and loving, but they have no religion at all. Are they all going to hell or to purgatory? That's a grisly scenario! Couldn't they at least go to limbo?"

"Limbo? Where've you been? We don't have limbo anymore. The church did away with that years ago. Limbo's not even mentioned in the new catechism."

"Oh, well, maybe by the time we die they will have done away with purgatory and hell too, and then we can all go to heaven and live happily ever after."

"In your dreams! Purgatory . . . hmmmm . . . maybe. But hell, never! Hell is here to stay. My mom tells me Jesus mentions the word hell fourteen times in the Bible. Somebody's going to hell. I sure don't want to be in that number. Personally, I plan to spend eternity playing the accordion in heaven."

"Wait a minute. Are we talking about the same place here? There will be no accordions in heaven. If you want to play the accordion, you'll have to go to hell."

"What? No accordions? What's Lawrence Welk going to do for all eternity?"

"Honestly, Jolee, get a little class. You'll be playing for royalty. Have you ever seen a symphony orchestra with an accordion section?"

"If one of the requirements for entrance into heaven is good taste, you better find a home for those pink furry slippers. You'll never make it as a fashion consultant for the celestial elite."

"Where I go, my slippers go," I said. "You know I never have to dust my hardwood floors."

We chuckled and hugged affectionately. Jolee's visit had literally been a sweet treat. "Seriously," she said, heading out the door, "if there's only one way to heaven, I want to know it. . . . If they ask you to lunch, will you go?"

"Probably. I admit I'd like to ask questions, but I'd feel more secure if you were with me. I'll see if I can wrangle an invitation for you too, if you'll come."

"You know I would. Right now I have to get home. I'm on call for the rescue squad today," Jolee said, clutching the beeper at her waist.

Little wonder she was up and about so early.

I wasn't sure what to expect from Betty. I had only met her a few times when we'd volunteered at the hospital together. The Christian business call wasn't long in coming. Betty had made a commitment and she was hot on my trail.

"Hi, Laurette; this is Betty Green. I'm having a couple of friends over for brunch next week. I've been thinking about you and I was hoping you could join us."

("So I hear," I thought to myself.)

"Pat Frank will be here. You remember her, don't you?"

"Oh sure," I said, trying to sound surprised. "My friend Jolee and I went to a Bible study that Pat was teaching."

"That's what she said. If Jolee would like to come with you, I'd love to have her also." Betty responded just as I'd hoped. "All right then, we'll see you next week."

I didn't mention my upcoming rendezvous to the kids. They were not around much these days. Sometimes this once chaotic, noisy house seemed strangely quiet. All the children were growing up and establishing a life of their own. Some of them had moved a distance away. David was a freshman at Rutgers University, so he came home relatively often.

Before leaving for Betty's on Monday morning, I decided to wash my hair at the last minute. Lydia had been visiting for the weekend and left her auburn-tinted shampoo in my shower. Without reading the fine print, I lathered my (supernaturally) blonde hair generously and wrapped it in a towel to dry.

Looking in the full-length mirror twenty minutes later, it was hard to distinguish which end was up. I had my beloved pink furry slippers on my feet, and now I had pink furry hair on my head. I looked like a double-ended dust mop. I had to be at Betty's in twenty minutes. There was only one thing to do. I dug out my old "Eva Gabor" wig which always made me look more like "Nanook of the North" than like Eva Gabor. I had no choice. It was either the dust mop, or the Alaskan husky look. I tearfully chose the latter.

41

Jolee picked me up at 10:30 a.m. She came directly from an emergency call on the rescue squad. She smelled like the county hospital. "I don't have time to go home and change. They'll have to take me as I am. Having a bad hair day?" she asked, staring at my very unbecoming coiffure.

"Trust me, it doesn't get any better. Do you have to wear that hospital smock?"

"Let's just go and hope they can see beyond our dazzling exterior."

Betty's home was a miniature version of "Tara" on a southern plantation. The long, winding tree-lined driveway led to a magnificent columned home with colorful chrysanthemums in full bloom all around. There was a vine-covered gazebo in the side yard. Nearby, horses grazed lazily in a large enclosed pasture. I almost expected to see a heavy-set nanny open the extravagantly carved double front doors and announce our arrival to the sophisticated hostess: *"Mrs. Nanook of the North and Mrs. Florence of the Nightingale!"*

(One of us would probably trip over the threshold and end up prostrate in the polished foyer entrance. At least Jolee was dressed to cover any emergency.)

Betty looked a little like a cross between Scarlett O'Hara and Mother Teresa. Her tall, slim figure was draped in a flowing blue robe. Her shiny dark hair framed an aging face graced with more than a few wrinkles. There were candles and fresh flowers on the table and gold charger plates under the luncheon plates. Betty had prepared a flawless cheese soufflé that would make Julia Child look like a novice. The fruited Jell-O ring was a work of shimmery art in the center of a green lettuce wreath. Everything looked too perfect to eat. In the background we could hear the sound of rich, unfamiliar piano music. The only thing missing was the ice sculpture in the shape of an angel and flowing with pink champagne (probably an oversight).

Pat Frank had already arrived. She was as sweet as I remembered. There was something radiant and appealing about her. Betty's other friend was none other than Vickie, the movie star. I felt like I'd been set up for the kill. Jolee and I were like two little onions in a gardenia patch.

Lunch was scrumptious. The conversation was pleasant and non-threatening. Everyone just exchanged information about their families. Pat was a dental hygienist married to a dentist. They had two children of their own and had taken in twenty-two foster children over the years. The movie star turned out to be a widowed mother of three who worked as a fitness instructor to make ends meet. Betty gave piano and voice lessons at home in her spare time. Vickie, Pat, and Betty all attended the same church.

When the dessert arrived, swimming in a gooey chocolate sauce, I thought, "This must be heaven, and these three women have been sent to personally escort us to the kingdom of God. And me without my pink furry slippers!!!"

"Have you ever attended our church?" Vickie asked as I was savoring every delicious calorie, hoping they wouldn't show up on my body for at least a few hours.

"I haven't, but you have, haven't you, Jolee?"

"Just for a funeral once," Jolee answered politely.

She had a little chocolate sauce on her upper lip. When I tried to bring it to her attention by pointing to my lips, she responded with a smile. (Maybe she was right; she'd play the accordion in heaven.)

"We're having a one-day seminar at our church in October. It's about Jesus and his love through us, to others. We have an out-standing speaker and musician. She's an author and speaks all over the country. They're expecting a few hundred people. We'll all be there. Would you like to go with us?"

Here was our cue. Jolee and I both jumped in like we'd rehearsed but forgotten who had the opening line. "What about Jesus being the only way . . . *Jesus being the only way*?" Our voices blended together to give an echo effect.

Pat's face lit up. This seemed to be the opening she had hoped for. The sound of our words was still lingering in the air when she quickly answered our question with a question of her own. "Are you asking for yourself or are you concerned about others who perhaps don't know Christ yet or have never accepted him?"

"Well, let's take the Jews, for example. They don't accept Christ, but a lot of them are wonderful people. What about people all over the world who were taught that there are many ways to God? What about them? Are they all going to hell? That doesn't seem fair. Isn't that a little narrow-minded?"

"Absolutely! Absolutely! It is narrow-minded. Truth is narrow by definition," was Pat's surprising comeback. This woman oozed poise from every pore. "There's no question that it takes an uncompromising stand. But it's God's stand and he's in charge. He's probably the only totally fair judge we'll ever stand before."

"I don't understand that," said Jolee. She had licked the sauce off her lip now, giving herself a little more dignity and credibility. "If God is so fair, why would anyone go to hell? Didn't he pay the price for everyone?"

"Yes, he did," interjected Vickie, running her fingers through her long hair. ("I wish I could do that," I thought, "but if I did, I might accidentally pull my wig off. It wouldn't have the same effect.") "And when he did, he offered us the gift of eternal life. But not everyone wants to receive that gift. Some people receive it, look at it, and then toss it aside. They have no regard for the value of that gift and the price that was paid for it."

"But when you've been raised in a family and taught one way from the time you were born, how can you be held responsible for something you thought to be right all along?" I asked in a challenging tone. I'd heard these arguments before and I wasn't convinced of God's justice.

"God reveals himself to man in many ways," Pat answered. "We can see God in nature. Psalm 19 tells us, *'The heavens declare the glory of God.'* It says, *'Day after day they pour forth speech and night after night they display knowledge. There is no speech nor language where their voice is not heard'.* . . . In other words, even the heathen in the remotest part of the world can know God by looking at his creation.

"Listen to what the Apostle Paul tells us in the book of Romans: *'For since the creation of the world God's invisible qualities—his eternal power and divine nature—have been clearly seen, being understood from what has been made, so that men are without excuse.'*"

"Does she have the entire Bible memorized?" I wondered. That was a little unnerving to me.

"If anyone truly is seeking to find God, God will find some way to reveal himself to that person," Pat continued. "He says, *'If you seek me with all your heart, you will find me.'* Anyone who wants to know God needs only to seek the way that he provided, which is Jesus Christ. No one else ever claimed to be God. That's why he was crucified; and no one else ever rose from the dead. Why would anyone follow a God who has no victory over death?"

"I'm still not sure that it's fair to send people to hell for eternity because they've never heard the name of Christ," I continued to argue.

"Do you think it would be fair that everyone should go to heaven?" asked Betty.

"Well, maybe not everyone. I don't want a mass murderer in heaven. I'm talking about average people who are doing a lot of good things in this world."

"So God's measuring stick then should be the degree of sin or the amount of good one does to offset sin?"

"That might be fair. I don't want to see Hitler in heaven, but if God can forgive me, then why can't he forgive others too?"

"Well, of course he can. He's sovereign. He can do whatever he wants. What we have to remember is that he is a meticulously just God. He doesn't judge like the world judges. He's very far above that," Betty said as she brought out a fresh pot of coffee.

I had recently given up smoking and was still going through withdrawal symptoms. Coffee was a definite association. Jolee shot a glance my way when she saw me holding a paper-wrapped, after-dinner mint between my fingers like a cigarette. "Would you like a light for that?" she asked kiddingly.

"No. The last time I lit a paper mint I singed my bangs. With this head of hair I'm likely to burn the house down or start another fire like Mrs. Murphy's cow." I laughed, explaining to our hostesses what happened to my hair and why I was wearing this silly wig.

They all thought that was hysterical. Pat said she couldn't wait to tell her children the story. (I wondered how many phone calls she'd have to make to tell twenty-four children.) Vickie said she was so glad I didn't wear this all the time. She didn't think it was becoming at all. Betty insisted I give them a peek at my pink hair under the mop. "It can't be that bad," she exclaimed.

"Take it off, Laurette!!" Jolee encouraged me with a drum roll on the dining room table. "Ta de dum-Ta de dum-Ta de dum pum, pum! Ta de dum-Ta de dum-Ta de dum pum pum!!!!"

After the second drum roll, I whisked off my clever disguise in a theatrical gesture, and my bright pink pony tail went cascading down to my shoulders. I thought Pat was going to go into convulsions. "It really is pink!" she shouted between shrieks of laughter. "I can't believe it. I never saw anything sooo . . . soooo . . . pink in my life!"

Vickie was crying in her napkin after having sent a mouthful of coffee flying all over the table. "You look like a disheveled Easter bunny. Do you suppose it glows in the dark?" she howled.

Betty was slumped over the table making funny squealy noises. Jolee was making a cross-legged beeline for the bathroom, making "*ooh, ooh, ooh*" sounds all the way.

"And people wonder if Christians have fun," Pat commented, as she wiped the tears from her eyes. "I don't know when I've ever seen anything so funny."

The gales of uncontrollable laughter started all over again when I thought it was time to cover my sin by putting the wig back on my technicolor head.

"Why don't you leave that thing off?" Betty said. "You'd

probably be more comfortable. How will you ever get that color out?" she asked, trying to be sympathetic, but still attempting to suppress the giggling.

I was beginning to feel like a stand-up comic. If nothing else, my misfortune had been good for a laugh. Somehow the whole mood had become more relaxed. The discussion didn't seem quite so intense. Everyone had let her guard down. Now we were friends who could be real and open with each other.

Pat very determinedly brought the conversation back to where we had left off. "We were talking about degrees of sin," she said. "But God who is holy says he can't even look upon sin, any sin. Sin will not be allowed in heaven. If we could bring sin into heaven, then we would just be transferring earth to heaven. So then heaven would be no different than what we have here."

"What about purgatory?" Jolee asked.

"Purgatory? The Bible never mentions any such place, either in the Old or New Testaments. Jesus never referred to any intermediate state for the soul. The Bible tells us that the blood of Christ cleanses us from **all** sin. There is no need for further purging. The belief in purgatory runs counter to all Biblical teaching of the final judgment."

"Then why do we pray for the dead?"

"We pray only for the spiritually dead," Pat replied, "those who haven't accepted Christ yet. We need to pray for their salvation. But after the death of their bodies, there's nothing more we can do. Salvation must be decided on this side of eternity."

"How can anyone ever be fit for heaven?" Jolee kept pressing Pat for answers.

"We can't. That's why Christ had to come to take our sin on himself. When we accept him, he takes our sin and sends his Spirit to live inside us. Then we have no sin because Christ took it all on the cross. No one else could do that, because no one else was sent by the Father, only the Son. Does that make sense to you?"

"Yes, but I'm still concerned about those who don't know him," I admitted.

47

"Gals, your salvation is between you and God. Why not leave those strangers in the hands of a just God who loves them and will treat them fairly. When you stand before God, it will be just you and God. You need to trust him to care for others and trust him for your own salvation."

All the giggling had ceased now and there was total silence. I'd never had it explained like this before. It was reassuring to me. It did make more sense than anything I'd ever heard.

"Hmmm . . . hmmm . . . " was the only intelligent comment that Jolee and I could muster.

"Listen to what Jesus says in the book of Matthew," Betty added. *"'O Jerusalem, Jerusalem, you who kill the prophets and stone those sent to you, how often I have longed to gather your children together, as a hen gathers her chicks under her wings, but you were not willing.'* . . . Jesus is saying that he's brokenhearted because the people will not come to him to be saved. He hasn't changed. It still breaks his heart. He says it's not his desire that any should perish."

"I heard a woman say on a TV show one time that there were many ways to God," I said very timidly. My argument was getting noticeably weaker all the time.

"Really?" Pat said. "That sounds like something someone would say on one of those talk shows. Oprah Winfrey is big on that kind of thing."

"Uh-oh." Now I really sounded like a pea brain. "It might have been on "Sixty Minutes' or 'Meet the Press,'" I answered cunningly. (That was a little white lie so it was just a small, insignificant sin. Or was there such a thing?)

"Yeah, that's it," Jolee said with a grin. "It was on 'Sixty Minutes' the day they interviewed Oprah Winfrey." She wasn't about to let me get away with prideful deception.

"You two really have fun chiding each other, don't you?" Vickie chuckled.

"We keep each other humble," I said lightheartedly. "Have some more chocolate sauce, Jolee." ("I hope she gets a big glob right on the tip of her nose," I thought. "See if I tell her.")

"The Bible doesn't indicate any other way for us to get to God other than through his Son, Jesus Christ," Pat said. "Jesus is the only provision God made to take our sin. Why should he pay the price and we give the glory to another?"

We gave our standard, brilliant answer, "Hmmm . . . mmmmm."

In the foyer the grandfather clock sounded a resonant chime: bong, bong, bong, bong. The cuckoo clock in the kitchen went off: cuckoo, cuckoo, cuckoo, cuckoo. I looked at my watch in disbelief. Where had the time gone? "It's three o'clock," Betty chimed. "I never adjust my clocks."

Vickie jumped up, "Oh, I have to pick up the kids at school. This was a wonderful time. Everything was absolutely delicious, like going to a fancy restaurant. I enjoyed getting to know you both a little better," she said, addressing Jolee and me. "Think about coming to that seminar. I know you'd get a lot out of it. But Laurette, try not to wash your hair that day. *Auf wiedersehen*," she chanted musically as she ran out the door.

Jolee and I extended our thanks to Betty and Pat, gave everyone a friendly hug, and headed home.

"They're beginning to make too much sense. It's a little scary to me," I admitted to Jolee.

"Remember what Walph Waldo Emerson said?"

"Walph who?" I mimicked. "You gotta do something about that. You just spent a fortune having your teeth fixed; now your tongue won't work."

"Ralph . . . Ralph . . . Waldo . . . Emerson," Jolee enunciated very slowly.

"Can you say Ralph Waldo Emerson fast three times?"

"Ralph Waldo Emerson . . . Walph Waldo Emerson . . . Ralph Raldo Emerson!" We were in stitches again; it seemed to be a chronic condition with us. What was it Pat had said about Christians having fun? We could do that.

"What did old Mr. Emerson have to say?"

"He said: 'A foolish consistency is the hobgoblin of little minds.'"

"Jolee, you are a fountain of trivia. I'm impressed, but what does it mean?"

"If you're smart enough (which is debatable), you ought to be flexible enough to have a change of mind."

"In other words, don't let foolish pride keep you from admitting you could be wrong?"

"You got it!"

"Thanks for the bit of philosophical wisdom," I said sincerely as Jolee dropped me off at home. *Merci mon amie. Au revoir.*

She threw a kiss my way and yelled, "*Arrivederci.*" We were so cross-cultural!

I was excited about some of the things I'd heard and I was eager to share them with John, but he called that evening to say he had a late appointment with a client. I picked up the *Good News Bible* that I'd bought and looked up the verse in Matthew that Betty had mentioned.

Matthew 25:37: *"O Jerusalem, Jerusalem, you who kill the prophets and stone those sent to you, how often I have longed to gather your children together, as a hen gathers her chicks under her wings, but you were not willing."*

The image of the mother bird covering her brood brought to mind the dove who had nested in my flower box last spring. At first she would fly away every time I approached the door. After the little ones were born, she refused to leave them even for a moment. One rainy night I spent five minutes securing a large umbrella over the nest to protect them. I was close enough to touch Mother Dove, yet she never moved. She was willing to risk her life to protect her brood.

For the next week or two I watched as Mother nurtured her two offspring. When the time came, she forced little Orville and Wilbur out of the nest onto my deck and very noisily gave them flying lessons. Wilbur was a quick learner and he proudly followed as Mother flew from the deck to the chair, to the table, to a nearby bush. Poor Orville, however, didn't fare as well. He stood and cowered in a corner. No amount of scolding or demonstrating by his mother seemed to calm his nerves. Orville clearly suffered from fear of flying, a very inconvenient obstacle when you're a bird. He fluttered his wings and tried to fly straight up but couldn't get more than an inch off the ground. Meanwhile, cocky Wilbur was showing off by practicing stunt flying right above him. By evening, Mother bird decided to teach Orville a lesson. She and Wilbur flew away and left little Orville quivering alone in a dark corner. They didn't come back till morning.

In the meantime, I tried to encourage Orville. "You need to get a running start," I said. I even tried cheering him on. "Orville, Orville, he's our bird! You say he can't fly, why that's absurd!" But Orville just sat there and trembled, not understanding a word I said. I wished I could speak *dove.*

Mother and Wilbur came back in the morning. She gently put her wings around Orville and seemed to whisper something in his ear. Orville straightened up, fluttered his meager feathers, and took off like a jet pilot. In no time, he was on the chair and then in the air. Orville made the decision. The only way is to trust and follow.

Mother had been kind, faithful, loving, and wise enough to discipline for Orville's best interests.

What a picture Jesus painted of his love for his people when he compared himself to the mother hen. How wonderful that he speaks our language so we can trust and follow.

*   *   *

Isaiah 53:5, 6   *But he was pierced for our transgressions, he was crushed for our iniquities; the punishment that brought us peace was upon him, and by his wounds we are healed. We all, like sheep,*

have gone astray, each of us has turned to his own way; and the Lord has laid on him the iniquity of us all.

John 10:9, 11 *"I am the gate; whoever enters through me will be saved. He will come in and go out, and find pasture. The thief comes only to steal and kill and destroy; I have come that they may have life, and have it to the full. I am the good shepherd. The good shepherd lays down his life for the sheep."*

John 10:28 *"I give them eternal life, and they shall never perish; no one can snatch them out of my hand."*

John 14:6 *"I am the way and the truth and the life. No one comes to the Father except through me."*

Acts 4:12 *Salvation is found in no one else, for there is no other name under heaven given to men by which we must be saved.*

Romans 1:18-23 *The wrath of God is being revealed from heaven against all the godlessness and wickedness of men who suppress the truth by their wickedness, since what may be known about God is plain to them, because God has made it plain to them. For since the creation of the world God's invisible qualities—his eternal power and divine nature—have been clearly seen, being understood from what has been made, so that men are without excuse. For although they knew God, they neither glorified him as God nor gave thanks to him, but their thinking became futile and their foolish hearts were darkened. Although they claimed to be wise, they became fools and exchanged the glory of the immortal God for images made to look like mortal man and birds and animals and reptiles.*

CHAPTER FIVE

Can I run the race in pink furry slippers?

As the holiday season was approaching, Jolee and I found easy excuses for not attending the seminar. We'd both accepted all the things we'd heard, but there was still some resistance. We still had some unanswered questions. With David and Valerie both away from home, and little contact with Pat or Betty, everything was easily put on hold.

As mid-December rolled around and all the children were planning to come home for the holidays, I was like a nervous hostess. Everything had to be just right. Decorations were all in place. Lighted wreaths, bells, bows, candles, the smell of fresh evergreens, and the glow of bright red poinsettias gave an unmistakable aura of Christmas. Presents were wrapped and under the tree to give a look of anticipation. The shopping and baking were finished. With a little effort, we would create an unforgettable memory.

The quiet that I'd quickly gotten used to would soon be broken with the sound of seven grown strangers who had been raised under our roof. They all had their own ideas and convictions which they loved to express. Hopefully, some of the things we'd taught them were still considered of value.

The Christmas gift I'd chosen for Dad was a 20" x 30" family photo to be taken in our home by Charles, the local photographer.

The children were all to bring home their Sunday go-to-church outfit. Judging from what they were wearing, some of them attended church in a wild jungle and others in the Waldorf Astoria.

"Valerie, aren't you allergic to that angora sweater?" I could hear a faint wheezing as she came bouncing downstairs, shedding fur with every step.

"Yes, if I keep it on too long. But how long can it take to have one family picture taken?" she asked.

"Matt, you're wearing holey jeans and you have no socks on!"

"I'll stand in the back. You'll only see me from the waist up. Is the sweater all right?"

"The sweater's fine. Get rid of the headband!"

Liz and Lydia had matching blouses and neither one wanted to change. "I had mine on first, Lydia. Besides, you brought your whole wardrobe with you. I only have three outfits. I'm not changing."

Lydia stomped up the stairs, pinching Liz on the way. She chose a bright red blouse which would clash completely with Liz's purple jumper.

"Oh no, now I'll *have* to change," said Liz. "You did that on purpose, Lydia."

"Hurry up, girls," the photographer said patiently. "My film disintegrates after three days."

Valerie's wheezing was getting louder and louder by the minute. "Call me . . . *wheeze* . . . when you're ready . . . *wheeze* . . . I'll be in my room . . . *wheeze*."

Jim showed up in a gray cashmere three-piece suit and paisley silk tie. He couldn't help it; he was born that way.

David was trying to get our Irish setter, Manfred, to sit. In ten years he'd never known what "sit" meant. Why would he think today would be any different? "Good dog," he said encouragingly. Manfred responded to his commands by scratching himself. "Good dog," David went on, undaunted. "Sit, sit, **Manfred, sit!** Oh, ugh, phew!!!! Dumb dog, get outta here!"

"Oh, yuk, I hope this doesn't show up on the pictures," Lydia laughed, as she frantically fanned the air. "We'll be lost in a purple cloud."

"Laurette, you don't really want to keep those pink furry slippers on, do you?" Charles asked in his stuffy nasal voice.

"Oops! Forgot I had them on."

Why couldn't we be like other families? Every year we got dozens of cards with family pictures. All of them looked like they'd been coordinated by a modeling agency. Children wore matching outfits; some wore Santa hats. They actually seemed to be having a good time. A few of them even had their eyes open.

Shortly after our photo session, the photographer sold his business and retired to Florida. He was only fifty-three.

With the photo shoot over, we could get down to the business of enjoying the time we had together as a family. One by one the kids began to rattle off the commitments they'd made with friends, and the people they planned to see over the next several days.

"Hold it!" Dad objected. "What about family time? Do your mother and I get to see you at all? Do we have to make an appointment?"

They all looked at each other with a common bond. "We'll be here Christmas Eve for the family dinner," the official spokesperson announced.

"And Christmas day, too, at least until noon," Peggy added.

For the next five days the lights never went out in our home. The last one in never knew if he *was* the last one in or not. (If I'd been smart, I would have put the whole house on the "clap on, clap off" system.)

When the phone wasn't ringing, it was busy. "Honey, we got a kid named Steve?" John asked in frustration at 11:00 p.m.. one evening when the phone had been ringing since 8:00 a.m.

"I don't think so, John, unless we've lost track of one somewhere along the way. The blonde, curly-haired kid with the pug nose isn't ours, is he? I think his name is Steve."

The cordless phone was a nightmare. Trying to answer it was like going on a scavenger hunt. *Ring . . . ring . . . ring. . . .* "It's coming from the sofa; look under the cushions! *Ring. . . .* I'm getting close; I can hear it. Don't hang up. *Ring. . . .* It's in one of the pillows! No?...Keep ringing, I'll find it. *Ring. . . .* Under the sofa! It's coming from under the sofa. *Ring. . . .* Here it is! *Hello . . . hello . . . hello . . .* They hung up."

When Christmas Eve came, Dad and I were intent on having our nest filled with all seven of our blessings.

"Hellooo!" I announced loudly over the intercom, having no mercy on those who'd chosen to stay out till dawn. "This is your mother. Remember me? I'm the one with the long, gray pony tail and the stretch marks on my stomach. I'm married to the redheaded man who lives with us. He paid to have your teeth straightened and your mind developed.

"We want to say 'Good morning.' We hope you've enjoyed your stay with us. If you should travel this direction any other time, we'd like you to consider our humble 'Bed and Breakfast' again. Thank you for your patronage. Dinner will be served precisely at five o'clock this evening in the main dining room. Attendance at dinner is absolutely mandatory for all guests of the 'Connelly Inn.' Dress code is semi-formal which, incidentally, is different from semi-dressed. Have a nice day and God bless us one and all."

"It's a miracle!" I heard John shouting a few minutes later. "Ma, look, it's the young'uns. They're all here at one time. Our babies have come home to roost. *Goool . . . lllly!* Fetch me the picture takin' machine, Ma! I want to get this on *fillum*!"

I looked up to find seven very sleepy, very grubby-looking kids standing in the hallway like a frightful mirage. One or two thought it was funny. The others were semi-comatose, but they all got the message. No one went out the entire day. Of course, the crippling blizzard pounding our area might have had something to do with that. I prefer to think it was their choice.

After setting the Christmas luminaries around the edge of the property, the three boys started rolling up snow to have a snowman contest. The girls were to be the judges. There was no guessing who built which snowman. Jim's ice sculpture was impeccably dressed in one of Dad's best ties and top hat; he carried a bulging briefcase. Matt had made a very well-endowed snow woman wearing a grass skirt, a huge rhinestone button for a navel. She wore a long, dark wig with a flower on top, and a lei around her neck. David's tall thin man had a Bible in his hands, and a smile on his face. He wore a foil halo for a headdress. Matt's snow woman won hands down. There was no contest!!

The dinner bell rang promptly at five o'clock. The table was set with the finest china we owned. A Hummel nativity scene served as a centerpiece. Dad gave the usual blessing: "Bless us, oh Lord, and these thy gifts which we are about to receive from thy bounty through Christ our Lord. Amen."

Our neighbors, Kathy and Dick Wilson, joined us for Christmas Eve dinner, as they had done for a number of years. The Wilsons were in their mid-fifties. Kathy was a bit of a prima donna who liked to give the illusion that she was closer to forty. You could almost feel the breeze from her false eyelashes when she blinked. (How did she manage to keep those things in place so perfectly? I would have had them floating in my soup or attaching to the little screws on my eyeglasses when I blinked.) Dick was generously overweight, but he preferred to think of himself as undertall. "I'm just big boned!" he liked to proclaim with assurance.

Dick treated Kathy like she'd hung the moon and called the stars out at night, each of them by name. The Wilsons had never had children of their own. Spending a little time with us now and then took away any regrets they might have had. At least they always left with a happy smile on their faces.

Before Dad had a chance to pop his annual question, "What are we most grateful for in the past year?" Jim got us started on a long unexpected discussion.

"David, you won't believe this. Your snowman is out there trying to convert Matt's snow woman."

"He's an evangelist. What can I tell you? He's probably telling her how God said 'the people of Canaan will melt away.' That gets snow people excited every time. Or maybe he's reading the Christmas story from the book of Luke. After all, it's a Christmas Eve tradition, isn't it?"

"My snow woman won't be easily persuaded," Matt replied. "She's a Jehovah's Witness. She doesn't celebrate Christmas."

"Maybe it would be a good idea if we read the Christmas story tonight. We used to do that when you were little, remember?" Dad was hoping to get to the real meaning of our gathering for celebration.

"Do me a favor, John; wait till after we leave," said Kathy with a little condescension. "I'm not sure I believe in God." Apparently she felt the children were now at an age when she could feel free to express her true feelings. She was very aware that some of them had more than a passing interest.

"Then why do you celebrate Christmas?" Lydia asked boldly.

"I don't; I celebrate the Festival of Lights."

The Wilsons had just returned from a one-year assignment in the Caribbean. "Do you mind if I have an after-dinner drink? We brought a bottle of Grand Marnier."

"I didn't know you felt that way," Matt said. "Weren't you raised in the church?"

"Yes, but now I can't help thinking, if God is real, why is there so much suffering in the world? Why so much hatred everywhere?" Kathy objected. She and Dick had done extensive traveling and she had strong opinions. "I've seen too much poverty and hunger. If God is so good, why doesn't he do something about the mess in this world?" She was looking around for an ash tray in what had become a smoke-free house. We pretended not to notice.

"This is not the world as God created it," David answered confidently. "We blame God for all our problems, but we've polluted our environment, the rivers, and the air we breathe.

Pollution generates disease. What's more, God gave us knowledge and wisdom and we use it to build bombs to destroy each other. Then we say, 'Why does God?' Isn't that a little unfair? Some day God is going to restore the world to what he originally intended it to be."

"Go for it!" I thought. "Stand up for God."

Liz joined right in to support David. "It seems to me that people cause most of the suffering in this world."

Wow! I could almost see my buttons popping.

"They have no value for life," she went on. "I don't know much about the Bible, but I believe God places a great deal of value on human life."

"Sure," Dick came to Kathy's defense. "People are guilty of causing suffering. But what about children who are born handicapped? What about earthquakes and hurricanes? They're not caused by people. Why does God allow things like that? Does he really care, or is he powerless to prevent suffering?" He was getting a little hot under the collar. "If God is all powerful, why doesn't he just wave a magical, holy wand or something and wipe out all the evil in the world?"

"First of all," David said, as he helped himself to a third piece of pumpkin pie, "if God chose to wipe out all suffering, he would also have to wipe out all the cause of suffering. There isn't anyone alive who isn't the cause of some suffering for someone else. That means we would all have to be wiped out. Wiping out the evil is not the answer."

"Then, what is the answer?" Kathy asked, almost apologetically, blinking her beautiful green eyes as she spoke. "I don't mean to be difficult, David, but when I look at my twelve-year-old nephew Paul, who has cerebral palsy, I can't help feeling that if God is real, he's cruel."

"I don't honestly know why some people suffer more than others. But I'm sure about this; God is sovereign. In his divine plan, he has a purpose for everything, including the earthquakes and even your nephew Paul."

"Isn't that blind faith?" Dick's voice bore a trace of sarcasm.

I wanted to come to David's defense, but he was holding his own.

"From the beginning man chose the path of sin. God created man with freedom of choice. He didn't make a bunch of robots or puppets that he could manipulate, creatures with no ability to love or make decisions on their own. We all would cry 'UNFAIR!' to that."

"Sure we would," Kathy agreed.

"But there are consequences to the choices we make. We choose to produce and sell alcohol," David continued. "People drink and drive and innocent people get killed. Then people say, 'God could have prevented it!' But if God intercepted the choices we make, where would our freedom be?"

"Smoking causes cancer, but people still want to smoke. They make a choice," Matt added. He was clearly on David's side. "If we stop the production of alcohol or tobacco or even drugs, people would be out protesting that their rights are being violated."

"I'm not talking about drunk drivers or smokers." I could sense a little hostility developing in Kathy's voice and I tried to give everyone a sign to ease back. "I'm talking about cerebral palsy, Down's syndrome, blindness, deafness, and on and on."

"We need to measure everything in the light of eternity," David responded, as gently as he could. "God originally intended that man should live in perfect health for hundreds of years. But now it's only his mercy that's made our lifetime very brief. He's anxious to take us out of this mess we've made to take us to the home he's prepared for us. He tells us that in the book of John."

"I have to tell you about a lady I met recently," I interrupted. "She and her husband have taken in twenty-two foster children over the years. Most of them were born addicted to alcohol or crack cocaine. Some were born HIV-positive. Those children suffer because of the direct result of poor choices by parents."

"So again, it goes back to ramifications. Innocent people suffer because people have chosen to do things their own way instead of

God's way." Valerie was cleaning and stacking dinner dishes as she spoke.

"Children shouldn't have to suffer because adults make mistakes." Kathy was clearly getting adamant.

John had always been convinced that when the family, or the smallest unit, fell apart, the country would not be far behind. This was a hot issue for Dad and he could never talk about it without becoming emotional. He was a family man with a strong sense of family values.

"This is one sick society," he said with authority. "Divorce is rampant, the suicide rate is sky high. Children are hooked on drugs. Young teens are having babies because they think it's cute. We have violence in our schools and gang members killing each other on the streets. Kids don't know the love and strength of the family anymore, because our concept of family is all messed up. We've redefined family and left God out of the equation! That causes a lot of suffering. But we can't blame God for the mess we've made. It probably breaks his heart to see the way we treat each other down here." Dad was getting visibly sentimental as he spoke.

There was silence in the Connelly home for at least ten seconds (a new record) while we all looked at Dad with fresh admiration. Except for the risk of embarrassing our guests, we might have given him a standing ovation.

Kathy extended her glass for a refill of the Grand Marnier. I'd never seen her speechless before.

"We've seen an awful lot of poverty and injustice in our travels," Dick informed us as he poured another one for Kathy and himself. "It's hard to reconcile that with a God of love."

"I believe that," I said. "But, I'm still convinced that most suffering is caused by other people. Think of the way certain ethnic groups have been treated over the years. And the agony we inflicted on African Americans in this country when we held them as slaves. We treated them as less than human, and we called ourselves civilized. Man's inhumanity to man is staggering."

Jim, always the tactful politician, sensed the conversation was getting a little heated. "Hey, it's six thirty. We better get those candles lit by the sidewalk. Who's gonna help?"

"We all will," John said. He quickly ran to help Kathy with her coat. "I hope we didn't come on too strong. When this family is united for a cause, we're like a brick wall."

"Hey, I started it," Kathy acknowledged. "You know what they say about not liking the heat."

"Yeah, let's all get out of the kitchen," one of the girls quickly agreed, leaving the dinner mess behind.

Outside we could hear the sound of Christmas carolers drawing near. We opened the front door to see a group of parents and children all bundled up with stocking caps, mittens, and mufflers. Flashlights covered with red crepe paper reflected on their excited faces as they serenaded us with the familiar Christmas songs.

"Mild he lays his glory by, Born that man no more may die, Born to raise the sons of earth, Born to give them second birth. Hark, the herald angels sing, Glory to the new-born King."

Kathy's face was aglow with delight. She seemed to truly enjoy the season. But what had made her such a cynic? I could almost hear myself in her persistent questioning. I wasn't there yet, but surely God had brought me a long way. As I watched Kathy fighting back the tears, I knew that behind all that skepticism was a seeking heart. A heart that wanted someone to convince her that God existed, and that he cared.

I wondered if she paid attention to the words the carolers were singing and if she understood them. . . . *"Light and life to all he brings . . . Risen with healing in his wings . . . Born that man no more may die . . . Born to give us second birth."*

"What joy and hope is ours if only we can believe the promises of Christ!" I thought. I had come a long way!

"Merry Christmas!" the carolers called as they shuffled through the mounds of snow. Some of them were being pulled on sleds. "I love your snowmen!" one of them hollered. *"We wish you a*

Merry Christmas, We wish you a Merry Christmas and a Happy New Year! Good tidings to you and all of your kin." We could still hear them singing after they were far out of sight.

The Wilsons had once or twice accompanied us for the 10:00 p.m. Mass. But this year they chose to leave for home before we had a chance to invite them.

We got through the Christmas holiday and one by one, the children went back to work or school and the place they now called home. David would still be around till the end of January.

After the first of the year, Kathy stopped by one afternoon to return something she'd borrowed from me. "Do you have time for a cup?" I asked.

"Sure, I've just spent a couple of hours grocery shopping and running errands. I need a break."

She looked more like she'd just been to high tea at the Helmsley. I wondered if she slept with those eyelashes on. Didn't they come off in her sleep now and then and settle under her nose somewhere like a little Hitler mustache? Careful, Laurette, don't slip and ask "milk and sugar in your eyelash?" I tried to stifle a giggle as these thoughts invaded my mind.

"So what are you doing with yourself these days, Kathy?"

"Oh, I've just been busy de-decorating. It takes me days to take all the lights down. I have to get it done this week because we leave for winter vacation in about ten days."

"Oh, that's right. Where will you be going this year?"

"Skiing in the Swiss Alps. I can't wait. That's one of our favorite places to visit. I know you don't ski, but have you been to the Alps yet?"

"No, I don't like heights. I don't even like being this tall," I said with tongue in cheek. *(Have I been to the Swiss Alps? Does she have a clue of what education costs for seven kids? I was still waiting to catch a blue light special at K-mart so I could buy a new toaster and she was talking about the Swiss Alps . . . Get real!)*

"You're so funny," Kathy snickered. (Kidding with her was no fun at all. She just didn't seem to get it.)

We sat cross-legged on the loveseat, her beige suede Gucci shoes swinging restlessly. "Don't those look comfortable!" she mused, eyeing my well-worn pink furry slippers.

"I have to wear them. They're prescription slippers!" I said. "Milk and sugar in your uh . . . uh . . . in your coffee?"

"No thanks. You know, Laurette, I truly enjoyed the discussion we had on Christmas Eve. I hope you didn't mind that I mentioned my feelings about God in front of your family."

"Not at all. A few years ago I might have minded. But the kids are old enough now to stand on their own convictions. I've gotten so I love to hear the depth of their beliefs."

"I wish we'd had time to address the natural disaster problem. You know, floods, earthquakes, hurricanes," Kathy went on. "I'd like to hear what David's explanation would be. He's really gung-ho about this religion thing, isn't he?"

"He wouldn't agree with that at all. He tells me it's not about religion. It's about trusting in Jesus Christ alone for salvation. I'm just beginning to understand the difference."

"Well, I would call him religious."

"Kathy, you and I were religious. We grew up with lots of religion. My religion did have some impact on my life and surely gave me an awareness of God. But it never penetrated every aspect of my being like the Bible has done for David and Valerie. We had a set of rules to live by. These kids have faith in the God of the Bible. They have something you and I know nothing about. I've learned a lot in the last few years. Some of it took a while to sink in. But you know I'm a little dense at times."

"That's very interesting. Maybe we'll have a chance to talk again sometime," Kathy answered.

"David should be back any minute. He just ran to the store for me. I know he'd like to see you. He's always ready and willing to talk about Jesus."

"Maybe another time," she said, quickly gulping down her coffee. "I better get home before my ice cream melts. It's not very cold out there." She was out the door as fast as her Guccis could take her.

David pulled in the driveway as Kathy was pulling out.

"Was that Mrs. Wilson? She was in a hurry!"

"Yes, and guess what. She thinks you're religious."

"Mrs. Wilson doesn't know where I'm coming from," David remarked as he was unpacking bags of groceries.

"I sent you out for bread, eggs, and milk and you come home with four bags of groceries?"

"Mom, I'm going to be home for two more weeks. I need junk food! What did Mrs. Wilson have to say?"

"She was hoping that someday she might get your perspective on natural disasters. Why does God allow them and all that." I was watching him in disbelief as he emptied the bags. "You bought three bags of Oreo cookies?"

"Four. I ate one bag," David confessed sheepishly and quickly tried to rationalize his actions. "They were on sale. Actually, I didn't eat the whole bag. I gave a few to a couple of cute, little kids. I knew you'd want me to do that. You always said 'nothing's worth having if you can't share it.' What's for dinner?"

"Why don't I just give you thirty-five dollars and let you go to McDonald's?"

"Let's see, thirty-five dollars. I should be able to get six all-beef patties, special sauce, lettuce, cheese, pickles, onions on a sesame seed bun, three large fries, two apple pies, and three cokes. Yeah, I think that would do it."

"Oh, lead me to the vomitorium!"

"You want me to be strong, don't you, Mom?" David picked me up and spun me around in the air, sending my precious slippers flying in every direction.

"Strong . . . yes; dead . . . no!" I said, retrieving my pink furry slippers at either end of the kitchen.

"Anyway, Kathy left very quickly when I told her you'd be home soon. I think she really wants to know truth, but she's afraid of it. I remember feeling the same way not too long ago."

"I don't have any of the answers Mrs. Wilson wants to hear," he said, taking a crackly bite off a shiny McIntosh. "I'd have to tell her the same thing I've already told her. We live in a fallen world where sin is glorified. It's not what God wanted for us; it's an abnormal world and it won't be normal again until he comes back."

"Until he comes back?"

"Yes, you know he *is* coming back. Till then, he's not nearly as interested in our happiness as he is in our salvation. One is temporary; the other is eternal."

"I never thought about that. I expected he'd want us to be happy here and now."

"I'm sure he would love that for us. But that's not the ultimate goal. Happiness is circumstantial and people affect our circumstances. I'm not God, and I don't know all the answers. All I know is what he tells me in his Word. God doesn't expect anything from us that he himself didn't endure. He didn't spare his only Son from suffering. Why should he spare me? Isn't it enough that Jesus died because he loved us? Who do we think we are to question God?"

Now it was my turn to be speechless. I had received enough information in the last few years to make a difference in my life. I'd held back long enough; it was time to accept and believe. Still, my stubborn heart resisted for a few more weeks. Something always stood in the way of decision making.

It was February before I finally surrendered my life to the One who knew me and loved me before I was born. I attended a meeting at my church in preparation for Lent. A visiting priest and a layman were speaking.

"You have to ask Jesus to come into your life and be your Lord and Savior," they said. There seemed to be no conflict with what I'd heard from others so often in the past few years. As they spoke, I could almost feel a burning in my heart, like there was an urgency about the things I was hearing. I knew I couldn't put it off anymore.

After leaving the meeting, I sat alone in the cold, empty church parking lot, feeling very weepy for some unknown reason. I opened my prayer book and found a little prayer card that Pat Frank had given me months earlier. I fingered the card cautiously, allowing the tears to flow freely. I read and re-read the words. Everything within me seemed to be shouting, "Give in, Laurette! Give in!"

"Lord," I prayed, *"I know I'm a sinner and I need a Savior. Thank you that Christ died to pay the price for my sin. I don't know a lot about you yet. But will you please be my Lord and Savior and Master of my life? Amen."*

All the way home the tears came. I couldn't wait to tell John how I'd prayed, but he didn't feel well, and he'd gone to bed early. I climbed into bed, gave him a peck on the cheek, and went to sleep with an excitement in my soul. I would tell him about it tomorrow.

I felt like I was at the starting gate of a brand new track. The lanes were a little ominous to me. Where would they lead? But I was equipped with my favorite running shoes. On the brink of sleep, I mentally clicked my cozy, pink furry slippers:

"Lord, I do believe . . . I do believe . . . The way to my eternal home is to follow in the footsteps of Jesus Christ till I come to the cross and recognize the One who died for me."

*   *   *

Psalm 12:8   *The wicked freely strut about when what is vile is honored among men.*

Isaiah 55:8, 9   *"For my thoughts are not your thoughts, neither are your ways my ways," declares the Lord. "As the*

heavens are higher than the earth, so are my ways higher than your ways and my thoughts than your thoughts."

Jeremiah 16:12 *But you have behaved more wickedly than your fathers. See how each of you is following the stubbornness of his evil heart instead of obeying me.*

John 14:2 *"In my Father's house are many rooms; if it were not so, I would have told you. I am going there to prepare a place for you. And if I go and prepare a place for you, I will come back and take you to be with me that you also may be where I am."*

Romans 8:22 *We know that the whole creation has been groaning as in the pains of childbirth right up to the present time.*

Romans 11:33 *Oh, the depth of the riches of the wisdom and knowledge of God! How unsearchable his judgments, and his paths beyond tracing out!*

Revelation 21:1-7 *Then I saw a new heaven and a new earth, for the first heaven and the first earth had passed away, and there was no longer any sea. I saw the Holy City, the new Jerusalem, coming down out of heaven from God, prepared as a bride beautifully dressed for her husband. And I heard a loud voice from the throne saying, "Now the dwelling of God is with men, and he will live with them. They will be his people, and God himself will be with them and be their God. He will wipe every tear from their eyes. There will be no more death or mourning or crying or pain, for the old order of things has passed away." He who was seated on the throne said, "I am making everything new!" Then he said, "Write this down, for these words are trustworthy and true." He said to me: "It is done. I am the Alpha and the Omega, the Beginning and the End. To him who is thirsty I will give to drink without cost from the spring of the water of life. He who overcomes will inherit all this, and I will be his God and he will be my son.*

Chapter Six

Unscramble the letters to find something special.

"Kipn Sreppil Yrurf"

The next two years saw radical changes in the Connelly household. The major change was the death of my sweet husband, John. John became ill on February 17, the very day after I prayed to accept Christ into my life, in the church parking lot. He was gone eleven months later, at the age of fifty-five. Six months before his death John had also become a believer.

Spiritual growth was put on hold for over a year while I tried to just keep my head above water. At least, that's the way it seemed from my perspective. But I know it was not so from God's perspective. He was working in my life even through the hardships. If he was to make me into a new creation, he had a lot of work to do.

During those eleven months, Jolee, who had also made a decision for Christ, faithfully kept my spirits up by leaving constant little reminders of her love at my doorstep. There was something special in my mailbox every week. Sometimes it was just a single flower, or a balloon with a message, *"Hang in There."* It might be a jelly doughnut with a sweet note, or a silly puzzle to make me laugh:

(1)   FIND THE WORD "RED" IN THIS PUZZLE

bbbbbbbbbbbbbbbbbbbbbbbbbbbbbbbbbbbbbbbbbbbbbbbbbbbb
bbbbbbbbbbbbbbbbbbbbbbbbbbbbREDbbbbbbbbbbbbbbbbbbbbbbbbbbbbbb
bbbbbbbbbbbbbbbbbbbbbbbbbbbbbbbbbbbbbbbbbbbbbbbbbbbbbbbbbbbbbb

(2)   WHICH IS THE LONGEST LINE?

‗‗‗‗ ‗‗   ‐   ‗‗

_____

(3)   IN WHAT SPORT IS A TENNIS BALL USED?

Tennis_____ Football_____ Hockey_____ Golf_____ Swimming_____

(4)   CONNECT THE DOT

             •

(5)   CAN YOU IDENTIFY THE CITY WHERE THESE CAN BE FOUND?
        1 - Philadelphia Zoo _____
        2 - Boston Common _____
        3 - Los Angeles Freeway _____

        *   *   *   *   *   *   *   *

Give yourself 100 points for each correct answer.
        One thousand points   =   Genius
        Six hundred points   =   Extremely intelligent
        Four hundred points   =   Very smart

                (PS: I got them all right. Love, your genius friend, Jolee)

All the children finished college and either got married or
went off on their own. I was left alone with time on my hands. I
hadn't gotten very far from the starting gate of my new track. A few
high hurdles slowed my pace significantly along the way.

I still didn't have a clear understanding of what was expected
of me now that I'd become a 'believer.' But I had a vision. I would
write a book about John. Initially, I think I just wanted to keep his
memory alive for myself, my children, and all the grandchildren that

I knew would be coming along, sooner or later, never having known their granddaddy. I toyed with the idea for a while. When I got up enough courage, I rounded up all of John's medical records and began to pore over them. When I did, I had to deal with the pain and grief all over again. But once I got beyond that, I was able to write. I spent the next three and a half years writing the book entitled, *Where Are You, Where Are You Going, And How Are You Going to Get There?*

Sometimes writing seemed to be an impossible mission. I found myself lying in bed on sleepless nights, staring at the ceiling. In my frustration I was having imaginary discussions with God.

Laurette: *"Lord, I don't know if I ought to just give up on this book idea. Sometimes I think it would have been easier to build an ark."*

God: *"That's already been done. Keep writing. You can do it with my help."*

Laurette: *"I don't think writing is my gift, Lord."*

God: *"Moses didn't think he had the gift of speaking, but that didn't stop him from leading the exodus."*

Laurette: *"Lord, I don't mean to be irreverent, but couldn't you give me another gift?"*

God: *"What did you have in mind?"*

Laurette: *"Wellll, maybe the gift of music? I've always wanted to play the organ."*

God: *"You've already tried playing the organ. I still remember when you practiced. Even the angels were walking around here wearing ear muffs. I had less trouble parting the Red Sea."*

Eventually, I would fall asleep with a smile on my face and a renewed commitment to writing.

To my amazement, the book was eventually published and my life began to change. God did have a plan for my life all along.

Shortly after John's death, Valerie and I met for dinner at my favorite Chinese restaurant.

"You need to get some good solid teaching, Mom." As always, Valerie had brought a fresh supply of tapes for my listening pleasure.

"Why don't you try going to the chapel sometime to hear Pastor Leeds in person?" Valerie asked. "You enjoy his tapes so much and he'd like to meet you. He often asks how you're doing. I expect you'd enjoy going to that church."

"Go to a different church? You mean on Sundays? I can't do that! I'd feel like a traitor," I objected. "I wouldn't know what to expect, when to sit, stand, kneel, pray. I still don't know where to find things in the Bible. Besides, why would I have to leave my church?"

"You don't have to. God doesn't really care which church you attend. But it should be a Bible-teaching church because you need to grow in his Word. You just have to be willing to go where he calls you to be, that's all."

"The big problem I would have is with Communion," I confessed, as I relished every morsel of moo goo gai pan and egg foo young. "Does your church believe in the transubstantiation?"

"Trans what? I don't believe in anything I can't pronounce. What are you talking about?"

"You remember, don't you? In Communion we receive the actual body and blood of Christ? That's called the transubstantiation. The changing of the bread and wine into the literal body and blood of Jesus," I answered.

"I do remember that's what we were taught. But I never knew what that belief was based on, and I didn't know it had a name."

"Well, it's based on the fact that Jesus said, 'This is my body and this is my blood.' That's why it's called the sacrifice of the Mass. I do know some things about the Bible."

Valerie cringed at that one. "We don't literally eat him. We eat the bread and wine in his memory."

"In his memory, yes, but he did say, 'This is my body and this is my blood,'" I argued, determined to make a point.

"He also said he was the light, the branch, the rock, the vine, the gate, the door. But he didn't mean those in a literal sense. When he spoke to the multitudes, he spoke in parables," Valerie said as she opened up a fortune cookie.

"I don't claim to understand the transubstantiation, honey. It's a mystery. I've just always believed it. I believe that's how I receive Christ, through Communion when I eat his body and drink his blood."

"Okay, then how come we never got the wine? We always just took the bread. Even today, very few people take the wine. Does that mean they only get his body and not his blood? Who made that decision? What's a body without blood? It has no life. The life is in the blood!"

I signaled to one of the waiters for the check. This was my nickel and I would call the shots. It was easier to have this kind of conversation with strangers than with one of my children. Besides, I wasn't in the mood for confrontation.

"You received Christ when you asked him into your life as your Lord and Savior," Valerie continued. "He said he would never leave you nor forsake you. He's there to stay. He lives within you. He doesn't go in and out."

"I know that, but there are some things I really need to work through at my own pace," I said. "Are you coming back to the house or are you driving home tonight?" My voice had gone up a few decibels.

"I have to get home; tomorrow's a work day. You haven't opened your fortune cookie," Valerie reminded me, as she read from the wisdom of Confucius: "'Love is a forever thing.' Hmmm, that's just what I've been telling you."

"Listen to mine: 'You can't run your life on empty.' Wow! That's deep."

"Can I just say one more thing before we leave?" Valerie asked courageously.

"Talk. I have a feeling you will anyway."

"The Bible tells us that Christ lives in his resurrected body at the right hand of the Father and that his Spirit lives in the hearts of his children. There's no need for any further sacrifice. He died once for all."

"Uh-huh, is that it?"

"That's it," she said with a discouraged groan.

"Don't push me, Val. I promise to look into it sometime. Is that fair enough?"

"Fair enough." Valerie kissed me on the cheek and walked me to my car. "Love you, Mom; I'll call you over the weekend. Thanks a lot for dinner. Next time will be my treat."

I couldn't wait to go home to relax in front of the fireplace with no one lecturing me. My nerves were still pretty raw, and these discussions often left me feeling emotionally wiped out.

When I got home, Mighty Manfred, the wonder dog, was hiding under the bed shivering and whining. He'd had an accident by the front door—a frightened reaction to being home alone during a lightning storm. One foot on the wet ceramic tile sent me pirouetting in the air, like an awkward ballerina, before I landed on my backside.

"Manfred!!!" I screamed. "You are one step away from the pound!!"

At the sound of my voice, Manfred came barreling down to greet me, three steps at a time, his tail madly fanning the air.

"Woof . . . woof . . . woof!!" (Translation: *What are you doing on the floor? Oh, I get it . . . you're trying to teach me to roll over. . . . Give it up! I'm never going to roll over for a crummy cookie. . . . I'm not that dumb."*)

"Arf . . . Arf . . . Arf!" (Translation: *"Here, let me help you up."*)

One large paw extended in exuberant greeting had me down again while I struggled to get up.

"Bark . . . woof!" (Translation*: "Oh my, you're wet. Where've you been? I missed you. You're my best friend!"*) "Slurp . . . slurp . . . slurp!"

I remembered when we agreed to get a dog. Seven little people and one grown man promised with their lives to take care of him. They would clean up after him, feed him, train him to do simple tricks, like do his business outdoors. Where were the promise-makers now? They were all gone, and they left me alone with a thirteen-year-old paranoid, pedigreed piddler.

"Get off me, Manfred! Stop licking me! . . . Help!! I'm sitting in a doggie accident being licked by eighty pounds of matted fur with bad breath and gas!" I screamed. "Okay, okay, you're my best friend, too. Now move away and let me get up." (Translation: "You may never see tomorrow, you irresponsible canine!")

I got back on my feet and walked in the kitchen to find all my appliances shouting orders at me. The power had apparently been off for a while. The microwave was flashing: "Refer to manual and reset . . . Refer to manual and reset . . . Refer to . . . " The clock radio was blinking, "RESET . . . RESET . . . RESET." The dishwasher sign said, "Cycle interrupted . . . Cycle interrupted . . . Cycle . . . " The answering machine was blinking, "Messages . . . Messages." (So far, this was not a day I would place on my re-order list.)

"Whoever invented talking appliances never had kids or dogs," I thought. "I've had it. I don't take orders from appliances! I am the mistress of this house and I'm going to have the last word around here if it kills me!!!"

I marched defiantly upstairs to shower and change my soggy, smelly clothes. I put on my tranquilizing, pink furry slippers and warm, cuddly robe. Then I fearlessly stood in the middle of the kitchen. I looked right into the instrument panels of my appliances and at the top of my lungs, shouted belligerently and with absolute authority, **"I WILL NOT! YOU CAN'T MAKE ME!!!"** Then I went to bed without resetting a thing. (There is power in that kind of action.)

I overslept the next morning and was late for a meeting because the alarm wasn't set. It was a dubious victory, to be sure. But I'd made it clear to my appliances that I was in charge. I would reset only when I felt like it. (I felt like it the next morning.)

After going through the series of tapes Valerie had given me at the last meeting, I finally made an appointment to meet the man who had made such a difference in Valerie's life. Pastor Leeds seemed eager to talk with me.

"I was sorry to hear about your husband's death," he expressed genuinely. "Valerie tells me you're doing real well and even preparing to write a book."

"I'm still in the preliminary stages," I offered tensely. I knew that even my being there, on foreign ground, was breaking all the cardinal rules of my church. It was a sure sign that I was beginning to seriously question the validity of some of my beliefs. Clearly, I was a rebel!

Pastor Leeds was completely the opposite of what I'd expected. He was probably in his early fifties. I had envisioned a short, pudgy man with a "U" hairstyle. But he was very tall and quite handsome. He had distinguished-looking salt and pepper curly hair, and a deep dimple in his chin. His office walls were covered with pictures of his wife and family. The room was surrounded by unrecognizable maps and a myriad of books on the Bible, dictionaries, commentaries, and encyclopedias. As Pastor Leeds spoke, his entire countenance revealed an unpretentious man who was devoted to his ministry. He spoke of the Lord Jesus Christ as if he personally met with him every morning before going to work.

After our brief introductions, I told him how much I'd enjoyed his tapes and how I'd met with Pat Frank a few times. I confessed that I was beginning to feel compelled to do some digging until I found truth. Not what someone else perceived to be truth, but absolute truth.

"My knowledge of Scripture is virtually non-existent," I humbly admitted. "I do have a Bible and I'm reading. But, instead of coming up with answers, I seem to have more questions as I go along."

Pastor Leeds smiled warmly and assured me that questioning is always a good sign. "You can't arrive at truth unless you ask questions," he said. "Maybe I can answer some of those questions for you. Would you mind if we prayed and asked the Spirit's guidance before we talk?"

Tears welled up inside of me as he modestly prayed the most caring, personal, loving prayer I'd ever heard. When he finished he leaned back and looked at me with compassion, giving me the impression that he had all the time in the world.

My voice was trembling with emotion when I started to speak. Pastor Leeds, seeing my discomfort, took hold of my hand and gave me a reassuring squeeze.

"My big problem right now is with the transubstantiation. I know there's a difference of opinion and I'm not sure I can accept anything except what I've been taught. Receiving the body of Christ in Communion has always been such a source of strength to me. I want to know why there's disagreement on this issue."

"Well," he said, "let me tell you what I, as a pastor, and what this church, as well as most Christian churches, understand to be the teachings of Christ on Communion.

"Before we go to Scripture let me say this. Jesus said many things figuratively, such as: 'I am the Good Shepherd.' He didn't mean he was an actual shepherd. When he said, 'You must be born again,' he wasn't speaking of a physical birth but of a spiritual birth. he said he was the light of the world, and he said *we* are the salt of the earth. These are all figurative terms not to be taken literally."

Pastor Leeds opened up his Bible and gave me a copy to follow along with him. "Let's look at John 6:50-58, page 989," he said, and he proceeded to read as I followed:

"John 6:50-58, *'But here is the bread that comes down from heaven, which a man may eat and not die. I am the living bread that came down from heaven. If anyone eats of this bread, he will live forever. This bread is my flesh, which I will give for the life of the world. Then the Jews began to argue sharply among themselves, 'How can this man give us his flesh to eat?' Jesus said to them, 'I tell you the truth, unless you eat the flesh of the Son of Man and drink his blood, you have no life in you. Whoever eats my flesh and drinks my blood has eternal life, and I will raise him up at the last day. For my flesh is real food and my blood is real drink. Whoever eats my flesh and drinks my blood remains in me, and I in him. Just as the living Father sent me and I live because of the Father, so the one who feeds on me will live because of me. This is the bread that came down from heaven. Your forefathers ate manna and died, but he who feeds on this bread will live forever.'*

"Now, let's see what Jesus meant by that," Pastor Leeds went on. "Does he mean that we have to eat his body and drink his blood in a physical, literal way? The context makes it quite clear that to eat of him means to believe in him. Augustine said, 'Believe and you have eaten.' Jesus was pointing to his death on the cross when his body would be broken and his blood shed as a ransom for sinners.

"Now," Pastor said, "let's go back to the text, when Jesus says. 'The bread that I shall give is my flesh.' He's using physical things to teach spiritual truths. If they didn't eat his flesh and drink his blood, they would have no life in them."

Now I was really confused.

"Now let's look at verse 47 in the same chapter," Pastor suggested. "That verse says that he who believes in him has everlasting life."

"Hmmm...," I said, not completely convinced.

His secretary interrupted our conversation with a subdued knock on the partially open door. "Excuse me, Pastor Leeds, but do you remember there's a staff meeting at two o'clock?"

He smiled at her and said softly, "Tell them to go ahead without me." Turning towards me, he said, "I don't have anything more important to do today, do you?"

I could see why his congregation loved this man so much. He was there to serve and take care of needs. I was needy.

"Now let's look at verse 63," Pastor Leeds said, keenly sensing my hesitancy. "This is Jesus speaking, by the way: *'The Spirit gives life, **the flesh counts for nothing**. The words I have spoken to you are **Spirit** and they are life.'* Jesus is explaining that these words are not to be taken literally; they're Spirit and they are life.

"Our Lord was not speaking of a Communion service. He's speaking about those who accept his death on the cross. Communion is only a way of remembering what he did for us. It's a celebration of our salvation."

Verse 63 had taken my breath away. It was all coming to-gether. *"The words I have spoken to you are Spirit."* Of course, that made more sense than anything I'd ever heard. Suddenly it seemed crystal clear. I didn't need to eat his physical body to receive him into my life. *"The flesh counts for nothing,"* Jesus said. *"The Spirit gives life."* It's his Spirit that lives in the hearts of his people, not his body!!! His Spirit doesn't float in and out like a flighty ghost seeking greener pastures whenever I sin, leaving me uncertain of his presence at all times. No! He's here to stay. He lives within my heart!

I felt like someone had just come in and turned on a bright light. It's his Spirit that teaches us the things of God.

The tears were flowing freely now. I began to snivel and fumble around for a tissue. Pastor Leeds gallantly handed me a box of Kleenex.

"Laurette, have you received Jesus Christ as your Lord and Savior?" he asked gently.

"Yes, I have, but I have so much confusion. I'm not sure of anything. I really need some direction and teaching."

"One thing you can be positively sure of—if you've accepted Christ, you have eternal life. That's his promise."

"Just stay in his Word and he'll reveal himself to you. Listen to what he says in Proverbs 7, *'My son, keep my words and store up my commands within you. Keep my commands and you will live; guard my teachings as the apple of your eye. Bind them on your fingers; write them on the tablet of your heart.'*

"There are lots of people around here who would be willing to help you and to answer your questions, if they're able. When you're ready, let us know and we'll arrange for someone to call on you."

"I'm ready!" I said with an eagerness that surprised even me.

Pastor Leeds laughed a hearty laugh and suggested a number of commentaries to help me get started. He also loaned me a couple of books from his private collection. "This way I'll be sure to see you again," he said, only half kidding. "Please, come back."

He gave me a warm, firm handshake and sent me on my way with more love in my heart than I knew what to do with. I went home and read the verses I'd heard over again. *"The words I have spoken to you are Spirit and they are life."* With each reading I felt a freedom like a breath of fresh air. "Yes, Lord," I shouted prayerfully, "I am free. Free from the fear of being left as an orphan, without Christ, even for an hour. Free to question and seek. Free to worship wherever you call. Free to study your Word. Free to follow wherever you lead. Free to be all that you want me to be!"

*   *   *

Leviticus 17: 10, 11   *Any Israelite or any alien living among them who eats any blood—I will set my face against that person who eats blood and will cut him off from his people. For the life of a creature is in the blood, and I have given it to you to make atonement for yourselves on the altar; it is the blood that makes atonement for one's life.*

John 6:47   *"I tell you the truth, he who believes has everlasting life."*

John 6:49, 50   *"Your forefathers ate the manna in the desert, yet they died. But here is the bread that comes down from heaven, which a man may eat and not die."*

John 6:63   *"The Spirit gives life; the flesh counts for nothing. The words I have spoken to you are spirit and they are life."*

John 7:38, 39   *"Whoever believes in me, as the Scripture has said, streams of living water will flow from within him." By this he meant the Spirit, whom those who believed him were later to receive. Up to that time the Spirit had not been given, since Jesus had not yet been glorified.*

CHAPTER SEVEN

Can you make my pink furry slippers disappear?

"What's that medallion on your dashboard?" Steven asked as we drove together to a neighborhood Bible study.

Steven, a young man in his late twenties, was doing an internship at Chapel on the Square as part of his seminary training. He lived in my neighborhood and attended a bi-weekly Bible study at one of the pastors' homes. I'd been invited to join them several weeks earlier.

"Oh, that's Saint Christopher. He's the patron saint of safe travel," I said naively, "but I think he's been defrocked, relieved of his saintly duties. I guess I should take him down, but I feel like I'm pulling the pedestal out from under him. Poor Saint Christopher has been gracing the dashboard of Catholic automobiles for generations."

"Defrocked? You mean like stripped of his title?"

"Yeah, I think so. I'm not sure why, but there seems to be some question as to whether he ever really was a saint to begin with."

"Wait a minute! Back up. What do you mean? First, he was a saint and then he wasn't? I don't get it. What's your definition of a saint? And what is a patron saint?"

"A patron saint is someone you might have been named after. All Catholic children are named after a saint, someone you would

81

emulate and pray to for help. Then there are patron saints who have different assignments. Like Saint Anthony is the patron saint of lost articles. Saint Luke is for the medical profession. Saint Jude is my personal favorite; he's especially for hopeless cases. That's me. There's a saint for just about anything."

"And how do these saints get their assignments?" Steven asked in stunned disbelief.

"I don't know. You sure have a lot of questions for someone who's in seminary. What are they teaching you in those classes anyway? I'm supposed to be asking the questions around here," I said jokingly as we pulled into Pastor Bricker's driveway.

Steven quickly jumped out of the car and ran around to open the door on my side. His smile lit up his entire face and revealed the whitest, straightest teeth I'd ever seen. He didn't look at all like an aspiring pastor with his long curly blond hair, green eyes, and rugged build. "I'm glad ministers can marry," I thought to myself. "He's much too handsome and sweet to be single. What a waste that would be." Sort of like the cute priest we'd nicknamed "Father O'Shame-sy" because he looked like Gregory Peck. What a shame he would never be available to any of the single women who always hoped he would come to their home for annual parish visits. There was always a long line at Father O'Shame-sy's confessional booth and the women hung onto his every word.

Steven took my hand and helped me out of the car. "I want to talk to you some more about this saint stuff," he said. "I want to hear how you think people get to be saints and why you would pray to them."

"You'll have to take a number and wait your turn," I said as we walked up the flagstone walk. "There are a few other people waiting to talk to me."

Children dressed in Halloween costumes were running up and down the street ringing doorbells. "Trick or treat," they chanted, as the proud parents waited and watched protectively in the background. In the Brickers' front yard was a huge cornstalk and pumpkins everywhere. But there was a total absence of ghosts, skeletons, witches, tombstones, or spider webs.

Inside the cozy little Cape Cod house there was no trace of Halloween decorations. Several people had already arrived and were gathered in front of a roaring, crackling fire enjoying hot chocolate and muffins. There was so much chatter and laughing going on they hardly noticed our entrance. Jolee had been attending the study for the last two sessions, and she was right there in the midst of the crowd like she'd always been part of them.

Pastor Bricker, who preferred to be called Al or Pastor Al, was a man in his mid-forties. He was short and portly with very little hair on his head, but a mound of it over his eyes formed one long unbroken eyebrow. Large, horn-rimmed glasses sat on his very generous nose. There was a sparkle about him like he just enjoyed being alive.

His wife, Mildred, was an adorable pug-nosed, petite brunette with a magnetic personality. Together, they looked like a mismatched set. But it was obvious to everyone that they were a team. There was a chemistry between them that was contagious and pleasant to be around. Their teenage boys, Paul and Luke, seemed to have acquired their zest for living. The house was always buzzing with groups of kids in goofy hairstyles and braces on their teeth. They looked more like a lively rock band than part of the youth group at church.

The boys were on doorbell duty, handing out Hershey bars with Bible story cards attached to each bar. They had blacked out their two front teeth, dressed like hillbillies, and greeted every excited goblin with a toothless smile. "I have become all things to all men," Paul announced as one of the men chided them about taking part in a pagan holiday.

After one or two more people came wandering in, everyone began to settle down in the circle of chairs, the sofa, and even on the floor. There were people from age nineteen to ninety, but no one seemed to notice the age differences. They were all part of a large family. Pastor Al took prayer requests and opened the study in prayer.

The group had just finished studying the book of Acts and was now moving on to the book of Romans. Jolee and I had put little tabs on the pages of our Bibles so we'd be better able to find a specific book.

"We'll start by reading chapter one all the way through, and then we'll talk about what it says and how it relates to us today. Sally, would you start reading, and someone else can pick up where she leaves off until we get through the entire chapter."

Sally was an elderly lady and a nervous reader, her trembling voice getting softer and softer as she read till it was almost impossible to hear her. Steven picked up where she left off in verse 7. He shot a glance my way as he read, "To all who are in Rome, beloved of God, called to be saints . . . "

After we finished reading the chapter, one man remarked, "This is going to be a great study. If all I could own was one book of the Bible, this is the book I would choose. Theologically, I think it's the most important book."

"I think so, too," a young woman agreed. "It was probably the most influential book in my life."

"I would probably take the book of Hebrews," another one expressed with confidence, "because it's so unique and powerful. The superiority of Christ over all."

One after another, people began to pick their favorite book and why they felt it was so meaningful.

Jolee looked at me with a questioning smirk as if to say, "What are we doing here? We've gone from elementary school to university."

"I like the book of John," I said in an almost apologetic tone.

Jolee smiled sweetly and agreed. (It was an easy selection. Our choices were still limited.)

Mildred sensed our discomfort and kindly gave us her support. "Oh, I think you're right," she said. "The book of John is the basis of our faith."

"I knew that," I whispered to Steven, who was sitting on the sofa beside me.

He smiled and gave me a warm, reassuring pat on the back. He knew where I was coming from.

Paul and Luke were doing their best to keep the doorbell ringing at a minimum while the study was in progress. Now and then a few teenagers would get the upper hand and cause some disruption. One particularly raucous young couple, dressed as lesbian brides, blatantly carried a sign: *"The Bride and Bride."*

We all caught a glimpse of them when we heard the boys' noisy objections. Pastor Al immediately interrupted his teaching to pray for the protection of young people. Mildred and another lady were quietly sniffling, trying to hold back tears of sadness. The innocence of little ones in clown or bunny costumes seemed to be marred by the aggressiveness of liberalism.

Al brought us back to our study without any further fanfare. "Well, in fact," he said, "God must feel that all the books are inseparable. He refers to the entire Bible as one book in a number of places. He calls it the book of life. If we were to limit ourselves to an individual book, it would limit our spiritual growth. Let's look at what we've just read in chapter one and see what it's all about. First of all, to whom is Paul writing?"

"To all in Rome who are loved by God and called to be saints," a very young female voice quickly answered.

"Exactly," Pastor Al acknowledged. "And since Rome was a Gentile city, he was probably speaking to mostly Gentiles, though there were certainly Jews there too."

"Excuse me," I said, very sheepishly, "but what does 'called to be saints' mean? Was he speaking to a group of exceptionally holy people like teachers or priests?"

"Oh, no," he answered. "He's speaking to believers. A person becomes a saint when he or she accepts Christ as their Savior."

"I guess I'm thinking of a different kind of saint," I said. "You know, like Saint Paul or Saint Terese—proven saints, canonized saints."

"Okay, maybe we need to look at how one gets to be a saint and let's see if Saint Paul or Saint Terese are any different from other believers who are called saints."

"I always understood that a saint was a person who had led an exemplary life and maybe died for their faith," I said earnestly. "It used to be that in order to be accepted as a bonafide saint, one had to have performed at least two miracles. I don't know if that's still a criterion. But surely a saint who has been beatified and canonized is different from you and me."

"Miracles? I guess that lets me out," Jolee commented lightly.

"What? You don't do miracles?" I asked.

"I've been known to make a few people disappear. And I can do a few card tricks or sleight of hand, like finding a nickel in my ear. Does that count?" She was reaching into her ear and pulling out a small hearing device. "Oh darn. I always have trouble with this trick. I know that nickel is in there somewhere."

At this point everyone was laughing hysterically. It was good to know that we could be ourselves with them. There was no image of the somber Christian in this crowd. Even the ninety-year-old man was chuckling behind his impressive, bushy white beard.

Al brought us back to order. "The word 'saint' means 'holy people,' and it's a title for all God's people. It's true that people who were martyred for their faith during the early church were accorded special honor. But that honor often led to worship. The term 'saint' then came to be applied only to people of almost superhuman purity and goodness. But Biblically the term saint is correctly applied to anyone who believes that Jesus Christ is Lord."

"You mean like us?" Jolee asked skeptically.

"Just like us," Al affirmed. "Saints who often still give in to sin. But we have been sanctified by God."

I was beginning to squirm again. According to him, we were sitting in a room full of saints who were wearing blue jeans and walking shoes. That scene didn't fit in with my impression of what a saint should look like. All the saints I'd seen portrayed in galleries on convent walls had morose expressions on their faces and eyes rolled halfway into their heads. Some were bloody; most were crowned with shiny halos. My smiling face hanging in the midst of *them*, wearing a blue turtleneck and pearls, would have looked as out of place as it would in the Presidents Hall of Fame.

"Let's see how the word 'saint' is used in the New Testament," said Al. "In Acts 9:13, 32, 41, first Ananias and then Peter talk of the saints simply as believers in Christ. Paul continues this use in his Epistles to the Romans, Corinthians, Ephesians, Philippians, Colossians, Thessalonians, and Philemon. In each case saints seem simply to be people who name Jesus as Lord."

"You'd be hard pressed to convince my family that my patron saint, Joan of Arc, and I could be in the same category," Jolee objected. "I not only don't do miracles; I cower at persecution."

"I'll vouch for that," I said. "Forget burning at the stake. Pull her hair and she'll tell you everything she knows."

"You spoke about beatification and canon . . . something or other," Steven said, changing the course of the subject. "I'm slightly familiar with those terms, but they're not part of Scripture. I don't see those words anywhere in the Bible. Where do they come from? And what about sanctification?"

"I guess they come from tradition, and I don't know about sanctification," I answered with just a hint of irritation.

"I'm curious. What's a patron saint?" asked a sweet older woman.

I felt like I was on rerun. I'd just been through this with Steven.

"A patron saint provides a model and intercedes for us before God."

"Why do you need anyone else to intercede for you when you have Jesus?" Steven interjected. "The Bible says he's the only mediator between God and man. He's the only one who is able to intercede for us."

I was wide open to new teachings, but this probing was beginning to get under my skin. I was afraid of where this was leading. Would Mary be next? I knew this could be a dangerous area of conflict.

"I'm sorry, Al. We've obviously deviated from the lesson too long already. I didn't mean to send us into a long discussion," I said firmly, leaving no doubt in anyone's mind that this conversation was over.

Steven sensed that he'd made me uncomfortable and he gave me a precious apologetic smile.

"All right, let's get back to the lesson," Al said. "We're in Romans, chapter one. The purpose of the book of Romans is to present the clarity of the 'gospel' message. More specifically, it's a righteousness from God revealed in the gospel."

As Al went further into his lesson, he handed everyone an envelope, individually addressed. Inside was a bulletin labeled:

Good News

The key to Romans is found in Romans 1:16-17

Person of the gospel	Jesus Christ
Power of the gospel	Power of God
Purpose of the gospel	Salvation
For whom?	Everyone who believes
End result	The just shall live by faith

As Al elaborated on each one of these points, I could feel my spirit soaring with excitement. I had never heard the gospel presented in such detail and so personally before.

When the allotted time was over, I hated to see the session end. I was beginning to salivate after the knowledge of his Word.

"Laurette," Pastor Al said as I was getting ready to leave. "I'd like to meet with you and Jolee sometime and maybe go through some of the questions you might have."

"It seems to be what I do best these days," I said. "When you have free time call us and we can meet somewhere."

"You got yourself a date," Al said in his usual exuberant manner.

As we were leaving, the weather had turned unusually cold. All the pumpkins had been smashed into hundreds of slimy pieces, making the walk slippery underfoot. Steven practically carried me to the car, taking tiny baby steps all the way. He couldn't wait to apologize for having been a little pushy on the saints issue.

"I didn't mean to do that," he said. "I really am sorry. But I am interested in what you believe."

"I know you are, Steven," I answered emotionally. "When you speak about only one mediator, I know what's on your mind because David has spoken to me about that too. I don't mind talking to you about it. I just didn't want to discuss it with everyone there. But, I also know that I started it, so I guess I can say *mea culpa.*"

I could feel my eyes burning at the start of very unwelcome and embarrassing tears. Poor Steven felt guiltier with each warm flowing teardrop.

"Don't let the tears disturb you," I said. "I cry at supermarket openings."

"What can I do to make you feel better?" he asked pathetically.

His woeful plea was like a magic potion, turning my tears into laughter. "You didn't do anything to be sorry about. I told you I'm an impossible case. You can't take Saint Jude away from me. I need him to hold my life together."

Steven laughed nervously, making little hissing sounds through his pearly white teeth. I expect he was silently storming the gates of heaven: *"Help Lord! I'm just a kid; I don't know how to handle this weepy and confused old woman. Get me out of this mess!"*

On the front porch I could hear my telephone ringing while I fumbled to unlock the door. Before I could make my way to the desk, I heard the familiar voice on my answering machine: "Hi, Saint Laurette. This is Saint Jolee. Hey, I just realized tomorrow's All Saints Day. Since we've both just been sainted, doesn't it seem logical that we ought to celebrate? It's our birthday! How about tea at the Hilton at three o'clock? That would be a perfect atmosphere because they always have a harpist. We'll feel right at home. Call me."

"Only Jolee would think of All Saints Day," I thought. "She'll find any excuse for a party." The last time we went to tea we were celebrating the fact that her foot wasn't broken after she'd bought a piece of marble at a house sale and dropped it on her foot trying to get it into the trunk of her car.

After Jolee's call, the messages went on: "Hi, Mom, it's Lydia. Dan and I were talking about having Thanksgiving here this year. What do you think? Call me."

"Hi, Mom, it's Liz. I'm going to be home this weekend. How about garaging with me on Saturday? I need a few things for my apartment. Call me. I'm hoping Peggy will come too."

I'd call everyone in the morning. Tonight all I wanted was to watch the news and have a warm bath.

I plopped myself on the sofa and turned on the ten o'clock news. Manfred had settled down after giving me his usual exhilarating welcome. I gave him a little nudge in the nose with my stocking feet. "Manfred, fetch my slippers. Come on, boy, go. The pink furry slippers. You know the ones. Go get 'em, boy, go get 'em."

Manfred gave me a very faint "woof," lifted up his front paw, pulled it over his ears and buried his head deeper into his red beanbag bed. *"Get her slippers? . . . Ha! . . . I think not! . . . Hasn't anyone ever told her about letting sleeping dogs lie?"*

Manfred never let me down. He did exactly as any self-respecting, obedience-school dropout would have done. He'd failed to graduate not once, but twice. We finally gave up and decided he was not a prime candidate for higher education. John had hoped to train him as a hunting dog, but the only thing Manfred ever pointed to was a twenty-pound bag of Purina Puppy Chow.

The following day Jolee and I donned our most elegant "I've come for tea" clothes and headed for the Hilton.

We sat at a dainty little table overlooking the formal gardens. All around us were other dainty little tables with ladies celebrating one thing or another. On the loft sat a lady who could be none other than Rapunzel playing a golden harp like an angel at a royal banquet. Her long chestnut brown tresses cascaded down to her slim hips while her nimble fingers moved gracefully on the long melodic strings. Could this be a preview of "coming attractions"?

"Good afternoon, I'm Denise. I'll be your server today," said a shapely young lady dressed in a black, very mini tuxedo. "I'll give you a few minutes to look over the tea menu. Are you celebrating something special today, ladies?"

Jolee never looked up from the menu. "Okay," she said. "You be the server, and we'll be your customers. Yes, we're celebrating our sainthood. I'll have the orange spice tea, please."

Denise looked at her with a blank expression. "I'm sorry. I'm not sure I understood what you said you were celebrating."

"Our sainthood," I confirmed solemnly. "This is Saint Jolee and I'm Saint Laurette. I'll have the mint tea, please. And could you ask the harpist if she could play 'When the Saints Go Marching In'? That's our favorite song."

We both looked up in unison and smiled angelically at a very bewildered Denise, who was convinced at that point that we were both patients on furlough from the local institution.

Jolee and I would have been a good vaudeville team. One was always a lead-in for the other.

"So, Jo, how are you enjoying Pastor Al's teaching? I really love it. I'm amazed at all the things I didn't know."

"I know; I feel the same way. Although my mom's been trying to tell me for a long time, I'm beginning to understand her excitement. I loved the way he presented the 'Good News' last night, didn't you? That was so clear."

"Wasn't it?"

Denise brought our tea and a lovely tray of fancy little bite-sized sandwiches. "Where are you ladies from?"

"Paradise," I said, surveying the mouth-watering delicacies placed before us.

"Figures," said Denise. "Enjoy."

"Do you think she's a little confused?" Jolee asked. "Mmmm, try one of these little cucumber sandwiches. They're scrumptious."

"No more confused than we are. What do you make of all this saint stuff? Personally, I had less trouble acknowledging that I was a sinner than I do being a saint. That whole concept scares me just a little. I don't like putting myself on that level."

"I have to read more about that. But as far as praying to the saints, you know they do have a good point. Why should we go to all the saints when we can go directly to Jesus? The saints are just people like you and me. Except, of course, they died. But Jesus is God. And he did say, 'Come to me.' Not come to different saints."

"You've been talking to your mom, haven't you?'

"Last night."

"Does she consider herself a saint?"

"Absolutely! She gave me a number of verses to look up. I haven't had time to do that yet, but I will. . . . Did you taste the shrimp? Here, there's one left."

"When I die, will someone carve a statue of me to place on a concrete pedestal and light candles in front of it?"

"I don't think so. But if they did, Manfred would be quick to put the candles out."

All the refined ladies at the other dainty little tables were behaving like dignified 'ladies who lunch.' Jolee and I were slapping our laps and laughing hilariously. We were incorrigible. Even the Hilton at tea time had very little effect on our behavior.

"Excuse me, ladies. May I bring your scones now?" Denise interrupted, as she refilled our teapots. "How were the sandwiches?"

"Heavenly!" Jolee said.

"Good, and you're enjoying yourselves?"

"Oh, we're on cloud nine! Aren't we, Jo?"

Denise burst out laughing at that one. "I suppose you'll be wanting angel food cake instead of the usual petit fours."

"She's one of us, Jo!" I whispered across the table.

Denise was a good sport. From then on we were her favorite customers. I expected her to pull up a chair and join us when she brought the last course—a plateful of decadent-looking gourmet cakes and bon bons.

For the next hour we munched, licked our fingers, and chatted until almost everyone else had gone. "After you left last night, Al said he'd like to talk to both of us. He's going to call and set up a time. You know what that's leading up to, don't you?"

"Yeah, I know. My mom has been on my case about praying to saints for ages."

"It's not just the saints. The next step will be Mary. That's a real problem area for me. You know I've always been devoted to Mary. The Blessed Mother is the first one I've gone to for everything ever since I can remember."

"Maybe we need to consider that there could be something wrong with that," Jolee said seriously. "At least I'd like to hear what Al has to say about it. . . . Oh, my goodness. It's after five. I need to get home. Hank will be wanting dinner. He always does. What a drag! Why can't he eat out now and then like I do?

"I'm sorry," she said, spotting me wince. "That was thoughtless. I'm very grateful he's coming home."

Jolee was a winsome combination of fun, wisdom, and sensitivity.

Almost a year had gone by since John's death, but there were still lonely times, no matter how busy the hours were. The book was coming along very slowly. It was still only a step beyond the drafting stage. How could I apply myself to writing when my mind was still in such turmoil?

Sitting in Al's office a few days later, I was prepared to defend what I'd always believed. Jolee didn't have the background of parochial education that I did. She was more flexible and perhaps more teachable.

"I'm interested in your approach to saints," said Al. "You spoke about beatification and canonization. I did a little research on that and found that both are honors accorded by the church. In other words, the church, under the direction of the pope, decrees who is deserving to be called a saint. Are you with me?"

"I'm with you so far," I said, and Jolee echoed the same.

"That would mean that human beings can actually say that one person is more deserving than another to be in heaven because of the life that he or she led. Am I right?"

"So far."

"But the Bible doesn't speak of a need for beatification or canonization. It speaks only of God's sanctification of his children. The declaration of saints belongs only to God, not to man. Only God can judge the heart of man, no matter how wonderful he seems to be outwardly. In fact, Jesus told us that many would say, 'Lord, Lord, did we not prophesy in your name, and in your name drive out demons and perform many miracles?' He said he would tell them plainly, 'I never knew you. Away from me, you evildoers!' It's not for us to declare anyone holy. That's God's job."

"But we're called saints?" Jolee asked.

"We're called saints, but there again, only God knows those who are truly believers. We're told he sanctifies those who believe. *Sanctifies* means he makes them holy or saints. God calls all his children saints, not on the basis of what they've done but only on their belief in Christ. Jesus tells us, 'The work of God is this: to believe in the one he has sent.'"

"Then we're back to works, aren't we?" I asked.

"If our sanctification depends on our good works, yes; but it doesn't. It's all God's grace. We do the believing and God does the sanctifying."

Al handed us each a Bible. "Let's look up a couple of verses," he said. "Start with Acts 26:18." (That was a good place to start. I was familiar with the book of Acts.) '*"To open their eyes and turn them from darkness to light, and from the power of Satan to God, so that they may receive forgiveness of sins and a place among those who are sanctified by faith in me.'*

"1 Corinthians 6:11: '*And that is what some of you were. But you were washed, you were sanctified, you were justified in the name of the Lord Jesus Christ and by the Spirit of our God.'*

94

"Jude 1: *'Jude, a servant of Jesus Christ and a brother of James, To those who have been called, who are sanctified by God the Father and kept by Jesus Christ.'*"

"I love it!" Jolee shouted in her usual sparkling excitement.

"We could look up a dozen more verses," said Al. "But you see, it's God who makes us holy. That's what a saint is, someone who's been declared holy, not by man, but by God."

"Okay, I think I can accept that," I said genuinely. "But, if I know that someone is probably in heaven with God, why is it wrong to pray to that person to ask Jesus for something on my behalf?"

"Okay, good question. Let me ask you what you think prayer is?"

"Well, it's petition, it's invocation, talking to God."

"Right. It is all of those things, but first and foremost, prayer is worship. Worship belongs only to God. Let's look at the example of Jesus, who often went to prayer. He went always before the Father and prayed exclusively to the Father."

"I always felt that the saints had a closer connection and they could help me from heaven."

"The Bible is very clear on the fact that there is only one mediator between God and men, the man Jesus Christ. That means there is no other middle man, only Jesus. To go to a human being is to bring dishonor to his Name."

Jolee was easily convinced. "I think so," she said with assurance.

Al gave her a smile of approval and went on with his explanation. "We're also told that his Holy Spirit intercedes. The Bible says the Spirit of God helps us in our weakness. We do not know what we ought to pray for, but the Spirit himself intercedes for us with groans that words cannot express."

"Oh, then we have two mediators, Jesus and the Holy Spirit?" Isn't that a contradiction?" I asked rather timidly, not wishing to try Al's patience too much. Inwardly, I was hoping to poke a tiny hole in his theology.

"Remember that Jesus and his Holy Spirit are both part of the Godhead, along with the Father. They are one with the Father. All are one God. They're not separate deities. Don't ask me to   explain the Trinity. We'll never understand it on this side of eternity."

"Sounds acceptable so far," I admitted with only a trace of indecisiveness.

Al's face lit up with encouragement. "Every time we're told to pray in Scripture, it's pray to the Lord, pray to God, pray to the Father. Never, ever, are we told to go anywhere else or to pray to anyone else. We're told, 'Make your requests known to God.' Jesus said, 'Come to me. . . .' He said when you pray, pray like this: 'Our Father who art in heaven. . . .'"

"But aren't some saints working on earth now in the lives of people?"

"We know that God sometimes uses angels. But what the saints who have gone on to be with the Lord are doing right now, I'm not sure. I expect they're worshipping God. I don't have to know that. I just need to take God at his word. He says we can pray to the Father, Son, and Holy Spirit, and that's all. Pray to the three-in-one true God. Laurette, why would you want to go to anyone else when he's waiting to hear from you personally? He wants that personal relationship with you."

"Oh!" The light was beginning to come on. "That's how I can build a relationship with him. I think I'm beginning to understand. But what about Mary?" The words came out before I realized what I'd done. I couldn't believe that I'd brought the subject up myself after dreading it for so long.

"What about Mary?" Al repeated slowly and meditatively. "Okay, let's talk about Mary."

My throat was getting dry. I felt like I had just walked into a den of salivating lions without a weapon.

"May I put my feet on the sofa if I take my shoes off?" Jolee asked.

"Make yourselves comfortable. How about a cup of coffee?"

"Do you have anything cold?" I asked. "I'm really thirsty."

"Sure, no problem." Al left the office for a few minutes.

"Too bad you didn't bring your pink furry slippers. You could use the security right about now, couldn't you?" Jolee asked.

"Yes, but in a pinch you can be my security. Whatever you do, don't leave me alone with him."

In a few minutes we heard a quiet knock on the office door. Al had accidentally locked the door behind him.

"Who's there?"

"Al."

"Al who?" Jolee continued, playfully.

"Alleluia . . . Alleluia . . . Alle . . . eee . . . luuu . . . ya!" sang a loud baritone voice.

Jolee jumped up and opened the door to find a beaming Al holding a frosty pitcher of iced tea and a bag of chips with dip and cut-up fresh vegetables. When he laughed, Al's long bushy eyebrow seemed to flutter up and down like feathers in a breeze.

"Leftovers from the ladies' fellowship meeting this morning. This was good timing. **Party!!!!**"

"All right," Jolee said, having made herself comfortable on the leather sofa. "Bring on the entertainment."

Al did a little soft-shoe shuffle. "This is it," he said. "I don't get any more entertaining than this. What can I tell you? . . . Have some dip."

After a refreshing pause and a minute to settle down, Al was back on track.

His office door was wide open and in the background we could hear a heavenly choir practicing the most beautiful, peaceful music that made us want to sing along. *"Amazing grace, how sweet the sound that saved a wretch like me. I once was lost but now I'm found, was blind but now I see."*

"Now, about Mary. Unfortunately, Mary falls into two camps where churches are concerned. One church has placed her on such a high pedestal that she's actually, at times, obscured the vision of Jesus. That's a position Mary never sought, by the way. And I believe it would grieve her heart to know she'd been placed there."

"Oh . . . oh, here it comes," I thought. I could feel myself stiffen up.

"On the other hand, other churches, maybe because of fear of being drawn into the same situation, have chosen to completely ignore Mary. Two opposing positions, one as wrong as the other."

"Hmm, that is an interesting perception," I thought. I said nothing, but it pleased me to hear that the blame was not all one-sided.

"The Bible tells us that Mary will be called blessed among women. But how can we call her blessed if we refuse to mention her name? Somehow we've thrown out the baby with the bath water."

"I think you're right," said Jolee, munching on a crunchy carrot stick.

"We have to remember that Mary was chosen by God to be the earthly mother of Jesus. The angel said she was highly favored by God. That's the reason we should honor Mary," Al maintained.

"Yes!" I said. Heartened by his understanding, I gave him a thumbs-up sign.

Al smiled earnestly and went on: "We have a lot to glean from the woman named Mary. She was a perfect example of complete obedience to the will of God. She's very quick to say, 'Let it be done to me according to your will.' She's courageous. She has an unshakable faith. She trusts in the God who created her. She's a very special lady. But . . .," he added.

Oh . . . oh, that menacing little word "but" could spell trouble.

"Mary still needed a Savior like every last one of us. The Bible says there is none without sin. It clearly states, not even one. She was the very first person to call Jesus 'her' Savior in her beautiful Magnificat in the book of Luke. No one needs a Savior unless he or she is lost. Mary was saved by God's grace just like you and me. Again, it was man who bestowed the title of sinlessness upon her. That only happened in the mid-1800s. Mary herself never claimed to be without sin."

"But that's the Immaculate Conception. Are you saying that's not true?" I was beginning to feel on shaky ground. Jolee, on the other hand, seemed to be taking it all in stride. Why wasn't she defending her beliefs? Where was her loyalty?

"Laurette, God existed from the very beginning of time. He calls Himself '*I AM*' because before there was anything, *He Was*. God never had a mother but he chose a human being as a channel to bring the Messiah into the world. Mary was used by God to accomplish his purposes. She was very privileged in having been chosen and highly favored by God. But she was still a human being, a member of the sinning race. Nowhere in Scripture does it even hint at Mary being without sin."

Al spotted me fidgeting and sensitively touched my hand. "Don't take my word for all of this, Laurette. Study his Word and you'll come to truth. That's a promise from Jesus."

"I shouldn't pray to Mary?"

"You shouldn't pray to anyone but God. But you are free to love and honor Mary. You're free to glean important lessons from her life, like dedication, submission, contentment, acceptance, obedience, and on and on. When people pray to Mary, they give her the glory that belongs only to God. Prayer belongs to God and God alone."

"Jolee, you don't seem to have any problems with this," I said almost indignantly.

"I don't, but I come from a different background and I never felt the strong devotion that you did. This makes much more sense to me. If I'm going to believe anything, it will have to be the Word of God, not the dogmas and teachings of men."

"Amen!" Said Al.

I almost felt an alliance forming between Jolee and Al which made me even more uptight. She was supposed to be on my side.

"What about all the apparitions of Mary?" I asked. I was determined to grill Al till I knew he had no answer for me.

"Apparitions? What apparitions?" Al replied.

"Well, Fatima, Lourdes, and now Medjugorje. People who have been there say they've seen miracles. What's more, they say the vision is pointing people towards Christ. What do you make of that?"

"Laurette, that's not the way God speaks to us. Why would I need a vision when I have his Word and his Spirit living within me to reveal to me the things of God? We ought to be very leery of apparitions. Satan is very clever and he has a great deal of power. He can even perform miracles. What's more, he's most dangerous when he masquerades as an angel of light."

"Angel of light?"

"I'm not necessarily attributing these apparitions to Satan. I don't honestly know that. But I do know this—people can be easily deceived. That's why we're told to test the spirits. Even though a vision is pointing to Christ, where are people's eyes? They're on the vision. I'm not sure the Catholic Church has even acknowledged all of these apparitions. Do you know if they have?"

"No, I'm not sure," I answered feebly. "They must have approved of Fatima and Lourdes because churches are named after them. Also, the rosary and the scapular were given at the prompting of certain apparitions. There has to be some acknowledgment by the church."

"Okay, let's look in Scripture," Al said, as he always did, "and see what Jesus says about that kind of thing. Jolee, will you read Luke 11:29, and, Laurette, if you would read 2 Corinthians 11:14?"

"2 Corinthians 11:14: *'And no wonder, for Satan himself masquerades as an angel of light.'*" (Satan can take on any disguise. What could be more clever than taking the appearance of Mary?)

"Luke 11:29: 'As the crowds increased, Jesus said, *"This is a wicked generation. It asks for a miraculous sign, but none will be given it except the sign of Jonah."'*" Wow!

"The Bible tells us, *'The righteous will live by faith.'* It's our faith in Christ that makes us righteous before God. We're also told, *'Faith comes from hearing and hearing from the Word of God,'*" said Al with a sincere love that easily broke down all my resistance.

100

"I really need to know what the Word of God has to say. I can't understand why there's so much disagreement between denominations who all claim to use Scripture as their base," I said. "Why is that?"

"The difficulty is when you try to combine man's rules with the Word of God. That's when the confusion comes in. God gave us everything we need to know in his Word. To say that we can enhance it by human wisdom is unfathomable. To say that dogmas and decrees of men are on a par with the spoken Word of God is total deception. Jesus warned us about holding to the traditions of men and neglecting his Word."

Al was straightforward, but he constantly pointed us to the Word of God. He used no other books or sources of information to substantiate his position.

"Do you think there is deception in the Catholic Church?" Jolee asked boldly.

"There's deception of one sort or another in a lot of churches. Some churches pay too much attention to tradition. Others are too liberal and are quick to water down the Word of God to fit their own ideas of what they think is right. Some churches teach that salvation can only be through their own church. Still other churches settle for mediocrity; they become lukewarm in their dedication to Christ. In some instances we find corruption in the hierarchy of a church. That's why it's so important to be in a pure and vibrant church that reaches and preaches the truth of God's Word—a church with the spiritual vision that Christ has for his church. The 'universal' church of Christ has no denominational title. His church is made up of believers who are trusting in Jesus Christ alone for their salvation. It has nothing to do with a group of people who belong to a certain organized religion."

"That makes a whole lot of sense!" I had to agree. "I know when I spoke to Pastor Leeds I really felt the freedom to worship wherever God leads."

We had taken up a couple of hours on Al's day off, but he graciously made no attempt to cut us short.

"I think if I just continue to attend the Bible study and study on my own, I'll be able to work through some of these stumbling blocks that have been in the way of my understanding," I said.

"God will reveal his truth to you if you just seek it. That's his promise. If you have any questions, don't hesitate to bring them up at Bible study; or, if you prefer to ask privately, that's fine too. If you'd like Mildred to spend time giving you private discipling, I know she'd be glad to do that. Why don't we close in prayer now?"

As we walked out of Al's office, we came face to face with Pastor Leeds. He greeted me with a warm smile and an invitation to visit the church anytime.

"I think I'm going to do that very shortly," I said. "This is my friend, Jolee. We've both been attending Al's study for a few weeks."

"Great! Keep it up. Al needs someone like you to keep him on his toes," he said, patting Al affectionately on the back. "Let me know when you come for a Sunday service. My wife and I would love to have you over for lunch afterwards. You, too, Jolee. We just live down the street here."

"Man, these pastors sure are friendly and obliging," I said to Jolee as we sat enjoying spicy chili, refried beans, and burritos in a small Mexican restaurant decorated with fake cactus and beaded door-ways. "They always seem to have time to answer questions."

"Isn't that . . . *cough* . . . refreshing . . . *cough*?" Jolee gagged and quickly grabbed a glass of cold water to put out the fire of red hot pepper she'd just swallowed. "Wow! This stuff is . . . *cough* . . . lethal. It should be outlawed!"

"I know," I said. "That's what makes it so good. You're not supposed to eat those little red peppers. They're just for flavor and show."

"Then why are . . . *choke* . . . *cough* . . . they on my plate? My mother always taught . . . *humph, humph* . . . me to eat everything." I could almost see smoke coming out of Jolee's ears and her eyes were tearing like an open spigot.

"Fine. Here, take mine too," I said, piling all my fiery peppers on her plate.

"Are you okay, Señorita?" the flashy waitress asked as she refilled Jolee's water glass.

"Yes, fine. Could I have a little more hot sauce, please?"

In the midst of sizzling fajitas, three roving cabaleros clad in wide, colorful sombreros wandered around the gaudy dining room playing the violin. Adoring patrons, eager to be serenaded, discreetly vied for their attention.

"Jolee, don't do anything to attract them. I don't want them stopping here. If they do, I'm not looking up." (I knew as soon as the words were out, I'd made a dumb mistake.)

"*Cough . . . cough . . . cough . . .* Over here!" Jolee waved her arms frantically till the accommodating musicians began to stroll toward our table.

"You have a special request, Señorita?"

"I don't. But my friend does. What was that number you wanted to hear, Laurette?"

"I wanted to hear you choke!" I whispered between clenched teeth. "Have some more red peppers. I hope you swallow the crown on your front tooth!"

"Ah, 'Red Peppers,' si," the leader said with a friendly golden-tooth smile. "Amigos, 'Red Peppers,'" he said, pointing to his two companions. Right on cue, the two amigos began singing a very nostalgic "Red Peppers on Your Christmas Tree."

Jolee immediately went into the granddaddy of coughing fits till I was afraid she might need medical attention.

"We better get out of here before someone calls the paramedics," I said, grabbing our two cans of Diet Coke. "Let's go! We can finish these outdoors."

"I am . . . *cough . . . gag . . . choke . . .* the paramedics! . . . *cough.*" Between her gagging and coughing, Jolee was in hysterics again.

Once out on the walk, we sat under a giant plastic enchilada and tried to regain our composure. "'Red Peppers on Your Christmas Tree.' Honestly! Do you think they made that up?"

"I don't know, *cough* . . . but I'll never look at another . . . *cough* . . . Christmas . . . *hump* . . . tree again without seeing red peppers hanging all over it. Oh my, that ought to get us into the . . . *cough* . . . Christmas spirit."

"Uh-huh," I said pensively. The thought of my first Christmas without John could potentially send me into instant depression. I had tried not to dwell on it too much.

"How are you doing with that, by the way? Do you have plans for the holidays? This could be a tough one for you." Jolee's mood had suddenly changed direction when she sensed my apprehension.

"I'll get through it. Nothing could be as bad as last year. That was a devastating time. But I'm planning to enjoy this Christmas with my new grandbaby."

"That's the spirit! You've got a lot of livin' left to do, old girl. And you're gonna make it. Will you go to midnight Mass like you always have?"

"I don't think so," I said. "Valerie tells me they have a great candlelight service at Chapel on the Square on Christmas Eve. I think I'd like to go there."

"Really?"

"Yes. In fact, I'm planning to attend a Sunday morning service very soon."

"Wow! That's a major step. I guess Al really got to you today."

"It wasn't just Al. It's all the input I've received in the last few years. It all makes more sense than anything I've ever known. I told the Lord a long time ago that I wanted him in my life. But, it's hard to follow when you're not sure where he's leading and whether you really want to go there. There's always that little bit of resistance. I've especially resisted the term 'born again.' Somehow it left me with an uneasy feeling."

"You're right," Jolee agreed. "It seems to have a bad connotation."

"But you know, when Pastor Leeds used that term a few weeks ago, it wasn't a bit menacing. In fact, I remember that it was actually heartwarming."

"My mom has told me many times that it was Jesus who first used that term. She says that being born again means that you can see Jesus."

"I think your mom's right. I feel like I'm finally ready to take that first step to really follow after him. I'm a little shaky but I'm willing."

"Follow wherever he leads?"

"Wherever he leads!"

"Hmmm. You know what? I'm right with you. We really have something to celebrate about, don't we?"

There was a sense of a different dimension being added to our friendship. Jolee and I recognized that we were both on the verge of a new and exhilarating adventure. An adventure that would eventually lead us into different directions as we followed him.

"Cheers," we said, clinking our half empty Diet Coke cans. "To our new beginning." This was cause for celebration!

*   *   *

Romans 12:2 *Do not conform any longer to the pattern of this world, but be transformed by the renewing of your mind. Then you will be able to test and approve what God's will is—his good, pleasing and perfect will.*

2 Corinthians 3:18 *And we, who with unveiled faces all reflect the Lord's glory, are being transformed into his likeness with ever-increasing glory, which comes from the Lord, who is the Spirit.*

Romans 3:10   *As it is written: "There is none righteous, not even one."*

Matthew 12:48-50   *He replied to him, "Who is my mother, and who are my brothers?" Pointing to his disciples, he said, "Here are my mother and my brothers. For whoever does the will of my Father in heaven is my brother and sister and mother."*

Matthew 24:24   *"For false Christs and false prophets will appear and perform great signs and miracles to deceive even the elect—if that were possible."*

1 Timothy 2:5   *For there is one God and one mediator between God and men, the man Christ Jesus.*

Matthew 22:29   *Jesus replied, "You are in error because you do not know the Scriptures or the power of God."*

Mark 7:7-9   *"They worship Me in vain; their teachings are but rules taught by men. You have let go of the commands of God and are holding on to the traditions of men." And he said to them: "You have a fine way of setting aside the commands of God in order to observe your own traditions!"*

Matthew 6:6-9   *"But when you pray, go into your room, close the door and pray to your Father, who is unseen. Then your Father, who sees what is done in secret, will reward you. And when you pray, do not keep on babbling like pagans, for they think they will be heard because of their many words. Do not be like them, for your Father knows what you need before you ask him. This, then, is how you should pray: 'Our Father in heaven, hallowed be your name . . . '"*

Romans 10:17   *Consequently, faith comes from hearing the message, and the message is heard through the word of Christ.*

Proverbs 4:20-22   *My son, pay attention to what I say; listen closely to my words. Do not let them out of your sight, keep them within your heart; for they are life to those who find them and health to a man's whole body.*

John 6:45   *"It is written in the Prophets: 'They will all be taught by God.' Everyone who listens to the Father and learns from him comes to me."*

John 16:13-15   *"But when he, the Spirit of truth, comes, he will guide you into all truth. He will not speak on his own; he will speak only what he hears, and he will tell you what is yet to come. He will bring glory to me by taking from what is mine and making it known to you. All that belongs to the Father is mine. That is why I said the Spirit will take from what is mine and make it known to you."*

Isaiah 42:8   *I am the Lord; that is my name! I will not give my glory to another or my praise to idols.*

Chapter Eight

Hand me my pink furry slipper— I'm going to heaven!

The new beginning, I realized as I grew in knowledge and understanding, was a beginning that would never end on this side of eternity. Never end until his purposes have been accomplished in my life.

I'd had much confusion about the things of God, but one thing was clear: if I wanted to know God, there was only one place to start and that was in his Word. His Word was indeed a lamp unto my feet and a light unto my path. He gave me only enough light so I couldn't go ahead of myself or ahead of him.

It was never my intention to leave the comfortable, familiar church where I'd grown up. Originally, that possibility was not even an option to be considered. But if God was to do the leading, I had to be willing to let go of the things that held me back. It was almost like letting go of my mother's hand to walk on my own for the very first time. It was painfully difficult. I was wobbly, and more than a little fearful. I wanted to hang on tightly to just one finger on my mother's hand and without letting go, stretch to reach one finger on Jesus' hand. Maybe I didn't have to let go completely. Couldn't I just hang on to both and totter somewhere in between while they both supported me? But lovingly, Jesus stood with open arms only a few steps away. "Come," I could almost hear him say, as he encouraged me to take that first step. "Just keep your eyes on me and come. I'm here, I'll always be here. Don't be afraid. Come . . . come."

Leaving the church of my youth was by no means a flippant decision or an easy transition. I was well aware that there would be a price to pay, and there was. But his will had become my desire at any cost.

Chapel on the Square became my new church home. Pastor Leeds and his wife immediately took me under their wing and introduced me to different opportunities for learning and serving. Mrs. Frank, Betty, and glamorous Vickie were back in the picture with guidance and godly leadership.

Bible study at the Brickers' home became a real challenge and an avenue for spiritual growth. Jolee and I were becoming familiar with the different books of the Bible and even knew enough to make semi-intelligent remarks now and then (which was no minor miracle). We still managed to get ourselves into ridiculous situations at times. Our goals were changing, but our personalities were still unpredictable and maybe even bordering on the absurd. If God wanted us to be more solemn and dignified, eventually he would have to separate us.

That separation was not long in coming. Within a few months, Jolee's husband was transferred to a new station several hundred miles away and the painful parting began to take place.

"What do you mean you're moving? You can't go! I'm not finished with you yet!" I objected, as we sat in Jolee's immaculate, circular den having a cup of hot coffee and fattening glazed doughnuts. Jolee and Hank had the unenviable reputation of being Mr. & Mrs. Clean. While my fuzzballs were developing into beautiful works of art under my bed, hers were hunted down like choice prey. If there was any truth to the saying, "Cleanliness is next to godliness," they would be among the first in line for the kingdom.

"I've got news for you. God is not finished with either one of us. But I think he has a better chance of succeeding in making us holy if he splits us up."

"That wasn't part of the deal!" I bellowed. "I wanted us to grow holy together. Who will celebrate All Saints Day with me? Who will embarrass me in public? Who ... *sniff* ... will make fun ... *sniff* ... of my pink furry slippers ... *WAAAAAH* ... ?"

"I can still do that," Jolee was quick to affirm. But her teasing couldn't conceal the tears in her heart. "I tell you what. You give me one of your pitiful, dirty, moth-eaten, chewed-up pink furry slippers and I'll wear it when I feel lonely. You do the same with the other. Those slippers will remind us that our friendship is inseparable. We'll always be a pair, no matter how many miles come between us."

"What? After all the years ... *snivel* ... of making smart remarks, now you want one of my precious slippers? You gotta be kidding! You know ... *sniff* ... I plan to take those slippers into ... *blow* ... *honk* ... the kingdom with me, if the Lord will let me."

"No problem, you can bring your slipper with you when you go and I'll bring the other when it's my turn to go. We'll recognize each other immediately by the pink furry slipper on one foot."

"I don't know. I'll have to pray about that one. Couldn't I give you one of my old shoes?"

"Uh-uh ... it's the pink slipper or nothing."

"You drive a hard bargain! Have you put the house on the market yet?"

"Tomorrow, and don't you dare pray against a buyer."

"I wouldn't do that! I'll just pray that everyone who walks through this house can see that it's too dirty for human habitation. Is that all right?"

"That's fine," Jolee said, wiping a pea-sized smudge off the coffee table. "Want to go to the mall and ride the escalator? We could do a sing-along with the other riders."

Suddenly, the tears were flowing like a fountain. For the first time in our eighteen-year-old friendship, neither one of us could speak. This was going to be a very painful detachment for both of us.

Jolee's house was sold within a week and by springtime the moving van came to take my friend, her family, and all her belongings away from me.

As Jolee was packing the last bits of essentials in the car, I handed her a small box wrapped in pink foil and curly pink ribbons.

"I brought you something," I said with a lump the size of an orange in my throat.

"I'll take special care of this."

"Yeah, well, you have to promise me that you'll never wash it."

"I can't wash it? You must be delirious! You want me to live in the same house with this?"

"Listen, if it was dazzling clean like everything else you own, I'd never recognize it."

"All right, I promise. But it won't be easy!"

"It's not easy giving it away either! Remember, you have to take it with you when you go."

"I'll remember. I can see it now; I'm lying in a casket; all my friends are looking down at me saying, 'Doesn't she look like herself?' Instead of a lily, I'm holding on to a dirty, pink furry slipper . . . What's wrong with this picture?"

"Nothing's wrong. I like it!" I said with trembling voice. "It's you."

"Do me a favor, Teddy Bear, do something fun today, will you?" Jolee said as she tousled my hair with more gusto than usual.

"Hmmm . . . maybe, . . . maybe, . . . I'll go shopping for a new pair of slippers."

"Good idea! . . . I'll call you when we get there." Jolee and Hank blew me a kiss and left me standing teary-eyed in the driveway of their desolate-looking home.

God was filling my life with many new friends, but who could ever replace Jolee?

For months I spent hours in bed each morning surrounded by my Bible, commentaries, a Bible dictionary, a concordance, an atlas, maps and charts of Bible lands. This was a new expedition and I was determined to get it straight. I had to understand the correlation between the Old Testament and the New Testament. How did it all tie in together? It was like being on a treasure hunt, looking for the hidden things of God that I'd never known. Each new discovery was like opening a present from someone who loved me. Sometimes his love was overwhelming and tugged at my heart strings as I received gift after gift like a child with an indulgent parent at Christmastime.

For my part, I had nothing to give to him, only myself. But apparently that was all he wanted. My emotions seemed to vacillate from childish, spontaneous, unbridled joy and expectancy to uncertain tension and fear. Fear of losing what had become life and hope to me. Fear that he would be disappointed in me.

Months turned into years and all the time a slow transformation was taking place. God was busy refining some very rough edges in my life. In the process, even from the beginning, God was opening the way for me to share what little I knew with others around me. I had found a priceless gem and I was going to tell everyone about it whether they wanted to hear it or not. Sometimes my zeal was interpreted as enthusiasm, but more often than not, it was arrogance. I wanted to shake people and yell, "Are you blind? Why can't you see what I see? Don't you get it? Don't you know what's at stake? You really don't believe you're a sinner?"

Only a loving, patient God could gently remind me of where I'd come from. He could turn my foolishness into blessings, in spite of my "bull in a china shop" attitude.

Several years of training on the evangelism ministry served to soften my Christian witness. I began to see myself in other people, and my irritation turned to sincere, loving concern. I learned that I couldn't make people fall in love with Christ unless they could first see his love in me. Except for his love, I had nothing to offer them.

Commitment to daily, personal Bible study and prayer, as well as more structured group studies began to have a profound impact on my spiritual life. The more knowledgeable I became about Scripture, the more I realized how little I knew. I could consume all the doctrine in the world, but unless I knew Jesus, I was going nowhere.

It was that realization that began to strip me of the pride I'd had. I began to see how little I knew about a personal relationship with Jesus. Possibly how little I knew about myself and the condition of my own heart. If he was to do a work of regeneration in my life, God would have to make me look intently at all the nooks and crannies of my character and show me where changes needed to be made.

God led me into circumstances and situations that I didn't understand. All the time, he knew where he was leading. He had a plan for my life. It's only by his grace that I am what I am, a redeemed child of the King of Kings!

As I look back on my journey, I could never have fathomed his mercy or the depth of his love. He completely changed the direction of my life because he cared for me.

Work on my book continued. *Where Are You, Where Are You Going, And How Are You Going to Get There?* was completed and published at last. Publication led to television and radio appearances and eventually to very unexpected, unsolicited speaking engagements up and down the East Coast from Massachusetts to New York City to Florida and every state in between. In no time my calendar was overflowing with bookings for luncheons, seminars, and weekend conferences. His blessings have been overwhelming!

How can I keep track of all the opportunities God has brought my way? There is no yardstick long enough to measure his overabundant grace. Mercifully, I don't have to keep a running tally of my usefulness. I need only to treasure his desire to use his people as a channel of his love. The Holy Spirit will pour springs of Living Waters through any willing, yielded vessel. He is the power and the source of all successful ministry.

Family situations have changed. All seven children are married, and many wonderful grandbabies (thirteen so far) have brought much joy into my life. *(Prov. 17:6: Children's children are a crown to the aged, and parents are the pride of their children.)*

Lydia, Valerie, Jim, Liz, Peggy, Matt, and David have remained close to each other and to me, as a family. Though jobs or ministry have brought physical distance between us, some of the children are thousands of miles away. But I cherish the special occasions when they all descend upon me with their precious little ones, and once again turn my home into a boisterous "Bed and Breakfast."

I had expected that as I grew older, when all seven children were grown and settled on their own, I would move to a quiet farming community in Pennsylvania. There, I would take a new tranquility and enjoy a lull in the activities of the past forty years.

I *have* moved to a quiet place in Lancaster County, Pennsylvania, but I'm still waiting for the lull. At times I feel like a recycled antique. I'm showing a little wear and tear. You might find a dent here and there. But I've been reconditioned, I'm valuable, and I can still be used for his service. My prayer is that as long as I have breath, I will be available when he calls. He is King of Kings and will always be the Lord and Master of my life!

Three gaping holes remain in my life: Jolee, John, and one pink furry slipper. (Not necessarily in that order.) But I'm having so much fun with Jesus. Only he can fill all those empty spaces with his unfailing, everlasting love.

P.S.: If you ever run into a lonely-looking woman who looks spotlessly clean except for one dirty, pink furry slipper, give her a hug for me. But be careful about letting yourself get too involved with her. She can be charming and fun but she's just a little strange.

*　　*　　*

2 Corinthians 5:17   *Therefore, if anyone is in Christ, he is a new creation; the old has gone, the new has come!*

Jeremiah 31:3   *The Lord appeared to us in the past, saying: "I have loved you with an everlasting love; I have drawn you with loving-kindness."*